To

_____

From

_____

Date

_____

God's simple solutions

12 biblical principles for managing money

Freeman-Smith, LLC.
Nashville, TN 37202

The quoted ideas expressed in this book (but not Scripture verses) are not, in all cases, exact quotations, as some have been edited for clarity and brevity. In all cases, the author has attempted to maintain the speaker's original intent. In some cases, quoted material for this book was obtained from secondary sources, primarily print media. While every effort was made to ensure the accuracy of these sources, the accuracy cannot be guaranteed. For additions, deletions, corrections, or clarifications in future editions of this text, please write Freeman-Smith, LLC.

The Holy Bible, King James Version

The Holy Bible, New King James Version (NKJV) Copyright © 1982 by Thomas Nelson, Inc. Used by permission.

The Holman Christian Standard Bible™ (Holman CSB) Copyright © 1999, 2000, 2001 by Holman Bible Publishers. Used by permission.

The Holy Bible, New International Version®. (NIV) Copyright © 1973, 1978, 1984 International Bible Society. Used by permission of Zondervan. All rights reserved.

The Holy Bible. New Living Translation (NLT) copyright © 1996 Tyndale Charitable Trust. Used by permission of Tyndale House Publishers.

Scripture taken from The Message. (MSG) Copyright © 1993, 1994, 1995, 1996, 2000, 2001, 2002. Used by permission of NavPress Publishing Group.

The New American Standard Bible®, (NASB) Copyright © 1960, 1962, 1963, 1968, 1971, 1972, 1973, 1975, 1977, 1995 by The Lockman Foundation. Used by permission.

Cover Design by Kim Russell / Wahoo Designs
Page Layout by Bart Dawson

ISBN 978-1-60587-207-0

Printed in the United States of America

God's simple solutions

12 biblical principles for managing money

Table of Contents

Never spend your money
before you have it.

—

Thomas Jefferson

Introduction

A sound financial plan, like any good plan, starts with God. This book examines 12 timeless principles from God's Word about managing your money. These are principles that do not fail. And, thankfully, they are simple solutions: common-sense concepts for gaining and maintaining financial security.

The quest for financial security is—at least for most of us—largely a matter of applying straightforward lessons that are taught time and again in the Holy Bible. When we align our priorities with God's priorities, and when we apply God's teachings to every aspect of our lives, we prosper. But if we disobey God's commandments, or if we ignore Him altogether, we suffer the inevitable consequences of our actions.

God has a plan for your life that offers the promise of abundance and peace. Indeed, God has already chosen the path that He intends for you to take, but He won't force you to follow that path. To the contrary, your Creator has given you free will, the ability to make a wide range of choices about your spiritual and financial well-being. This book is intended to help you choose wisely. On these pages, you will discover Biblically-based resources that can assist you on the path to financial peace and spiritual abundance. And that, coincidentally, is precisely the path that God wants you to take.

Principle 1

Start by Putting God in Charge of Your Finances

Do not have other gods besides Me.
Exodus 20:3 HCSB

As you consider ways to achieve financial security, it's wise to place first things first, starting with God. Is God your top priority? Have you decided to give His Son your heart, your soul, your talents, and your time? Or are you in the habit of giving God little more than a few hours on Sunday mornings? The answer to these questions will determine how you prioritize your time and how you prioritize your life.

Whether you're at work, at home, or someplace in between, you're engaged in worship. In fact, all of mankind is engaged in worship—of one sort or another. Some people choose to worship God and, as a result, reap the joy that He intends for His children. Others distance themselves from God by worshiping such things as earthly possessions or personal gratification . . . and when they do so, they suffer.

In the book of Exodus, God warns that we should place no gods before Him. Yet all too often, we place our Lord in second, third, or fourth place as we worship the gods of pride, greed, power, or lust. When we place our desires for material possessions above our love for God—or when we yield to the countless temptations that surround us—we find ourselves engaged in a struggle that is similar to the one Jesus faced when He was tempted by Satan. In the wilderness, Satan offered Jesus earthly power and unimaginable riches, but Jesus turned Satan away and chose instead to worship God. We must do likewise by putting God first and worshiping only Him.

Is God in charge of your heart, your mind, your career, and your finances? Make certain that the honest answer to this question is a resounding yes. God must come first. Always first.

To Determine Who Is in Charge of Your Finances, Answer the Following True/False Questions

___ God is my ultimate financial advisor. I will trust Him with everything I have.

___ I understand the importance of being a careful steward of the money that God has entrusted to my care.

___ I will be generous with my tithes and offerings because I understand that everything I have ultimately belongs to God.

___ When I have a question about my finances, I'm willing to pray about it.

One with God is a majority.

Billy Graham

I lived with Indians who made pots out of clay which they used for cooking. Nobody was interested in the pot. Everybody was interested in what was inside. The same clay taken out of the same riverbed, always made in the same design, nothing special about it. Well, I'm a clay pot, and let me not forget it. But, the excellency of the power is of God and not us.

Elisabeth Elliot

When all else is gone, God is still left. Nothing changes Him.

Hannah Whitall Smith

God is an infinite circle whose center is everywhere and whose circumference is nowhere.

St. Augustine

Jesus Christ is the first and last, author and finisher, beginning and end, alpha and omega, and by Him all other things hold together. He must be first or nothing. God never comes next!

Vance Havner

Give God what's right—not what's left!

Anonymous

The Devil said to Him, "I will give You their splendor and all this authority, because it has been given over to me, and I can give it to anyone I want. If You, then, will worship me, all will be Yours." And Jesus answered him, "It is written: You shall worship the Lord your God, and Him alone you shall serve."

Luke 4:6-8 HCSB

Another also said, "I will follow You, Lord, but first let me go and say good-bye to those at my house." But Jesus said to him, "No one who puts his hand to the plow and looks back is fit for the kingdom of God."

Luke 9:61-62 HCSB

Be careful not to forget the Lord.

Deuteronomy 6:12 HCSB

Be still, and know that I am God.

Psalm 46:10 NKJV

For it is written, "You shall worship the Lord your God, and Him only you shall serve."

Matthew 4:10 NKJV

For the Lord your God is the God of gods and Lord of lords, the great, mighty, and awesome God.

Deuteronomy 10:17 HCSB

Pray About Your Finances

The intense prayer of the righteous is very powerful.
James 5:16 HCSB

Are you in the habit of praying about everything, including your finances? Is prayer an integral part of your daily routine, or is it a hit-or-miss activity? Do you "pray without ceasing"—as the Bible clearly instructs in 1 Thessalonians 5:17—or is prayer little more than an afterthought? If you genuinely wish to receive God's blessings, then you must pray constantly . . . and you must never underestimate the power of prayer.

As you contemplate the quality of your prayer life, here are a few things to consider:

1. God hears your prayers and answers them (Jeremiah 29:11-12).

2. God promises that the prayers of righteous men and women can accomplish great things (James 5:16).

3. God invites you to be still and to feel His presence (Psalm 46:10).

So pray. Start praying in the early morning and keep praying until you fall off to sleep at night. Pray about matters great and small; be watchful for the answers that God most assuredly sends your way; and don't be afraid to pray about your financial resources.

If you're uncertain about the ways that you're choosing to spend money, put your credit card back in your wallet until you've had a meaningful conversation with God. If you're thinking about changing careers, don't make a move until you've talked extensively to your Heavenly Father. If you want to make major changes in the structure of your financial life, ask God for the strength and wisdom to accomplish His plans. In short, pray often about the way that you earn and spend money. When you do, God will speak to you in the quiet corners of your heart, and as you listen and learn, you'll be rewarded.

Daily prayer and meditation is a matter of will and habit. When you organize your day to include quiet moments with God, you'll soon discover that no time is more precious than the silent moments you spend with Him.

The quality of your life is directly affected by the quality of your prayer life. So do yourself a favor: instead of turning things over in your mind, turn them over to God in prayer. Instead of worrying about your next financial decision, ask God to lead the way. Don't limit your prayers to meals or to bedtime. Pray constantly because God is listening—and He wants to hear from you. And without question, you need to hear from Him.

Never make an important financial decision or a big-ticket purchase without talking to God first.

Seek Spiritual Health First and Financial Health Second: To do otherwise is to risk God's disapproval.

Prayer is not an emergency measure that we turn to when we have a problem. Real prayer is a part of our constant communion with God and worship of God.

Warren Wiersbe

Allow your dreams a place in your prayers and plans. God-given dreams can help you move into the future He is preparing for you.

Barbara Johnson

Those who know God the best are the richest and most powerful in prayer. Little acquaintance with God, and strangeness and coldness to Him, make prayer a rare and feeble thing.

E. M. Bounds

My soul, hearken to the voice of your God. He is always ready to speak with you when you are prepared to hear. If there is any slowness to commune, it is not on His part but altogether on your own. He stands at the door and knocks, and if His people will only open, He rejoices to enter.

C. H. Spurgeon

Rejoice in hope; be patient in affliction; be persistent in prayer.

Romans 12:12 HCSB

Let the words of my mouth and the meditation of my heart be acceptable in Your sight, O Lord, my strength and my Redeemer.

Psalm 19:14 NKJV

Yet He often withdrew to deserted places and prayed.

Luke 5:16 HCSB

Don't worry about anything, but in everything, through prayer and petition with thanksgiving, let your requests be made known to God.

Philippians 4:6 HCSB

And everything—whatever you ask in prayer, believing—you will receive.

Matthew 21:22 HCSB

Rejoice always! Pray constantly. Give thanks in everything, for this is God's will for you in Christ Jesus.

1 Thessalonians 5:16-18 HCSB

Pray Early and Often

One way to make sure that your heart is in tune with God is to pray often. The more you talk to God, the more He will talk to you.

Sometimes, the Answer Is "No": God does not answer all of our prayers in the affirmative, nor should He. His job is not to grant all our earthly requests; His job is to offer us eternal salvation (for which we must be eternally grateful). When we are disappointed by the realities of life-here-on-earth, we should remember that our prayers are always answered by a sovereign, all-knowing God, and that we must trust Him, whether He answers "Yes," "No," or "Not yet."

Listen carefully—God is trying to get His message through . . . are you trying hard to hear Him?

Have you prayed about
your resources lately?
Find out how God wants you
to use your time and your money.
No matter what it costs,
forsake all that is not of God.

—

Kay Arthur

Notes to Yourself About Putting God First
and Praying About It

On the lines below, write down specific steps you can take to ensure that you keep God first in your life. Also, list specific aspects of your financial life that you need to pray about. This list might also include such things as your career, your future, your finances, your spending habits, or the general direction of your life.

_____

_____

_____

_____

_____

_____

_____

_____

_____

_____

_____

_____

_____

Principle 2

Seek God's Wisdom in Every Aspect of Your Life

Therefore, everyone who hears these words of Mine and acts on them will be like a sensible man who built his house on the rock. The rain fell, the rivers rose, and the winds blew and pounded that house. Yet it didn't collapse, because its foundation was on the rock.

Matthew 7:24–25 HCSB

The quest for financial security is a journey that leads us across many peaks and through a few unexpected valleys. When we celebrate life's great victories, we find it easy to praise God and to give thanks. But, when we find ourselves in the dark valleys of life, and when we face disappointments or financial hardships, it's much more difficult to trust God's perfect plan. But, trust Him we must.

As Christians, we can be comforted: Whether we find ourselves at the pinnacle of the mountain or the darkest depths of the valley, God is there, too. So, when we learn to trust God's wisdom and live according to His Word, we are secure.

Will regular readings of your Bible make you a financial genius? Probably not. The Bible is God's Holy Word; it is intended not as a tool for prosperity, but as a tool for salvation. Nevertheless, the Bible can teach you to become more moderate, more patient, and more disciplined. As you become a more disciplined person in other aspects of your life, you will also become more disciplined in the management of your personal finances—and the following common-sense tips can help:

- Enhance Your Earning Power and Keep Enhancing Your Earning Power. Opportunities to learn are limitless, and change is inevitable. In today's competitive workplace, those who stand still are, in reality, moving backwards . . . fast. (Proverbs 28:19)

- Live Within Your Means and Save Money from Every Paycheck. In other words, never spend more than you make. (Ecclesiastes 5:1)

- Use Credit Wisely. Don't borrow money for things that rapidly go down in value (furniture, clothes, new cars, boats, etc.). And if you borrow money for things that are likely to go up (like your home), borrow only the amount that you can comfortably afford to repay (in other words, don't "max out" your mortgage!). (Proverbs 22:7)

- Don't Be an Impulsive Buyer. Savvy salespeople want you to buy "right now." But savvy buyers take their time. (Proverbs 21:5)

- Don't Fall in Love with "Stuff." We live in a society that worships "stuff"—don't fall into that trap. Remember this: "stuff" is highly overrated. Worship God almighty, not the almighty dollar. (Proverbs 11:28)

- Make Sure That Everybody in Your Family Understands the Need to Spend Wisely. Within families, financial security is a team sport; make sure that everybody in your clan is on the team. (Matthew 12:25)

- Give Back to the Lord: God is the giver of all things good. What does He ask in return? A tiny ten percent. Don't withhold it from Him. (Malachi 3:10)

- Never Stop Studying God's Word. Even if you're very familiar with your Bible, there's always something new to learn. God still has many lessons to teach you . . . and you should be willing to learn. (Psalm 27:11)

Your Value System Will Determine How You Earn, How You Spend, and How You Save Money: So make certain that your value system is built upon the firm foundation of God's wisdom and God's Word.

God's principles of finance are no longer on trial; they have held true over the years.

Larry Burkett

Knowledge can be found in books or in school. Wisdom, on the other hand, starts with God . . . and ends there.

Marie T. Freeman

Having a doctrine pass before the mind is not what the Bible means by knowing the truth. It's only when it reaches down deep into the heart that the truth begins to set us free, just as a key must penetrate a lock to turn it, or as rainfall must saturate the earth down to the roots in order for your garden to grow.

John Eldredge

Wisdom is the God-given ability to see life with rare objectivity and to handle life with rare stability.

Charles Swindoll

This is my song through endless ages: Jesus led me all the way.

Fanny Crosby

But from Him you are in Christ Jesus, who for us became wisdom from God, as well as righteousness, sanctification, and redemption.

1 Corinthians 1:30 HCSB

For God has not given us a spirit of fearfulness, but one of power, love, and sound judgment.

2 Timothy 1:7 HCSB

Now if any of you lacks wisdom, he should ask God, who gives to all generously and without criticizing, and it will be given to him.

James 1:5 HCSB

But the wisdom from above is first pure, then peace-loving, gentle, compliant, full of mercy and good fruits, without favoritism and hypocrisy.

James 3:17 HCSB

A wise man will hear and increase learning, and a man of understanding will attain wise counsel.

Proverbs 1:5 NKJV

Teach me, O Lord, the way of Your statutes, and I shall keep it to the end.

Psalm 119:33 NKJV

Wisdom 101: If you're looking for wisdom (financial or otherwise), the Book of Proverbs is a wonderful place to start. It has 31 chapters, one for each day of the month. If you read Proverbs regularly, and if you take its teachings to heart, you'll gain timeless wisdom from God's unchanging Word.

How committed are you to God's wisdom? As a way of understanding your commitment level, answer the following True or False:

____ I continually remind myself of God's wisdom by reading the Bible each day.

____ I do my best to live wisely by obeying the teachings that I find in God's Word.

____ I associate with wise men and wise women.

____ I share my wisdom with friends and family members who seek my advice.

____ I do my best to apply God's wisdom to every aspect of my life, including my finances.

Examine Your Priorities

*And I pray this: that your love will keep on growing
in knowledge and every kind of discernment,
so that you can determine what really matters
and can be pure and blameless in the day of Christ.*
Philippians 1:9 HCSB

As you consider the way that you are currently managing your finances, take a moment to ask yourself this question: Are you investing your money on things that are pleasing to God, or are you wasting your money on things that are displeasing to Him? And while you're at it, ask yourself another question: Are you investing your life in a way that makes the most of the talents God has given you . . . or are you squandering those talents by allowing your skills to be underutilized?

If you sincerely believe that your spending habits are pleasing to God—and if you are firmly convinced that you're using God's gifts to the best of your abilities—congratulations! But, if your spending habits are undisciplined—or if your skills are not being maximized—it's time to rearrange your life and your priorities.

God has clear instructions concerning your spending habits: He wants you to be sensible. Proverbs 21:17 warns, "Those who love pleasure become poor; wine and luxury are not the way to riches" (NLT). God also gives clear instructions concerning your talents—He wants you to use them (Matthew 25). So the formula for financial health is straightforward: minimize unnecessary expenditures while maximizing your skills (and, presumably, your income).

If you're having trouble meeting the financial demands of life here in the 21st-century, perhaps you've organized your financial life according to your own desires, not God's. A better strategy, of course, is to take your daily obligations and place them in the hands of the One who created you. To do so, you must conduct your financial affairs in accordance with God's commandments, and you must seek His will and His wisdom in all matters. Then, you can face the coming day with the assurance that the same God who created our universe out of nothingness will lead you to a place of abundance and peace.

Do you feel overworked, under-appreciated, overwhelmed, and underpaid? Are your emotions (and your credit cards) maxed out? If so, it's probably time to reshuffle your priorities. And the best way to get started is by turning your concerns, of whatever kind, over to God—prayerfully, earnestly, and often. Then, you must listen for His answers . . . and trust the answers that He gives.

> Are God's priorities your priorities? And does your checkbook reflect your value system? If not, why not?

Your priorities, passions, goals, and fears are shown clearly in the flow of your money.

Dave Ramsey

Where your pleasure is, there is your treasure; where your treasure, there your heart; where your heart, there your happiness.

St. Augustine

Blessed are those who know what on earth they are here on earth to do and set themselves about the business of doing it.

Max Lucado

We set our eyes on the finish line, forgetting the past, and straining toward the mark of spiritual maturity and fruitfulness.

Vonette Bright

Since your personal value system will determine the quality and direction of your life, you must choose those values carefully; and you should choose them in accordance with God's commandments.

He said to them all, "If anyone desires to come after Me, let him deny himself, and take up his cross daily, and follow Me. For whoever desires to save his life will lose it, but whoever loses his life for My sake will save it."

Luke 9:23-24 NKJV

Let us fix our eyes on Jesus, the author and perfecter of our faith, who for the joy set before him endured the cross, scorning its shame, and sat down at the right hand of the throne of God.

Hebrews 12:2 KJV

Now it happened as they went that He entered a certain village; and a certain woman named Martha welcomed Him into her house. And she had a sister called Mary, who also sat at Jesus' feet and heard His word. But Martha was distracted with much serving, and she approached Him and said, "Lord, do You not care that my sister has left me to serve alone? Therefore tell her to help me." And Jesus answered and said to her, "Martha, Martha, you are worried and troubled about many things. But one thing is needed, and Mary has chosen that good part, which will not be taken away from her."

Luke 10:38-42 NKJV

For where your treasure is, there your heart will be also.

Luke 12:34 HCSB

Your Personal Mission Statement

It has been said, "If you don't know where you want to go, any road will take you there." Do you know exactly where you intend to go in life, and would you recognize your destination if you arrived there? If not, perhaps it's time to draft a clearly written personal mission statement.

How can we know the precise plans that God has for us? The answer, of course, is that we can't always know exactly where God wants us to go or what He intends for us to do. Even the most godly among us must struggle through periods of doubt and uncertainty.

Sometimes, outside circumstances will force us to reevaluate our lives; on other occasions, we may become frustrated, not by the turbulence of life, but by its sameness. In either case, we may find ourselves searching for new direction. If we are wise, we turn to God for that direction.

If you desire to make your own life a mission instead of an intermission, you should take time to write down your hopes, your goals, and your purposes for living. Drafting a personal mission statement can be a powerful way to clarify your thoughts and crystallize your plans. As you compose your mission statement, make it a concise document: keep refining it until it accurately reflects your life's purpose in as few words as possible. And above all else, make God your partner in every aspect of your life. God will hold your hand

and walk with you every day of your life if you let Him. So make your mission a mission for God. When you do so, your success is guaranteed.

Having values keeps a person focused on the important things.

—

John Maxwell

Notes to Yourself

On the lines below, make notes to yourself about specific ways that you can apply God's wisdom to the everyday realities of your financial life. As you're thinking about what to write, remember what God's Word says about such topics as debt, self-discipline, stewardship, and materialism.

_____

_____

_____

_____

_____

_____

_____

_____

_____

_____

_____

_____

Your Personal Mission Statement

In the space below, write a first draft of your personal mission statement. Don't limit yourself to financial matters. Instead, compose a brief synopsis of your priorities, your goals, and your purpose for living.

_____

_____

_____

_____

_____

_____

_____

_____

_____

_____

_____

_____

_____

_____

_____

_____

_____

_____

_____

_____

_____

_____

_____

_____

_____

_____

_____

_____

_____

_____

_____

_____

_____

Principle 3

Know Where You Stand by Making a Financial Plan

*Buy—and do not sell—truth, wisdom,
instruction, and understanding.*
Proverbs 23:23 HCSB

Do you want to improve the condition of your financial health? If so, here's a word to the wise: Start with a plan that makes sense to you and to God. An intelligent financial plan is an integral part of your long-term financial security. But planning is not enough; you must also be willing to stick with the plan you make. In other words, financial security requires intelligent planning and disciplined implementation.

Your financial plan is not merely a collection of numbers on a page; it is, more importantly, a reflection of your faith and your values. And, if you seek God's blessings, you will establish your plans in accordance with His commandments.

You've probably heard the song "My Way" (it was Frank Sinatra's theme song, and Elvis sang it, too). "My Way" is a perfectly good tune, but it's not a perfect guide for life here on earth. If you're looking for life's perfect prescription—if you're looking for joy, peace, abundance, and eternal life—you'd better forget about doing things your way and start doing things God's way.

God has plans for your life. Big plans. But He won't force you to obey His commandments; to the contrary, He has given you free will, the ability to make choices on your own. With the freedom to choose comes the responsibility of living with the consequences of the choices you make.

The most important decision of your life is, of course, your commitment to accept Jesus Christ as your personal

Financial Planning for Christians: Make all your plans—of whatever kind—with God's Word as your compass. If you're not putting God first, you're building on sand. And if you're building on sand, your building will crumble.

Lord and Savior. And once your eternal destiny is secured, you will undoubtedly ask yourself the question "What now, Lord?" And when you ask that question, you may rest assured that part of God's plan for your life includes a disciplined approach to your finances.

As a Christian, your financial plan should be an outgrowth of your commitment to obey God's Holy Word. As such, you must gladly offer God the tithe to which He is entitled (Malachi 3:10). If you intend for your tithe to be substantial, you should plan to maximize your income by continuing to improve your skills (thus improving your earning potential). Additionally, your financial plan should include provisions for insurance (life, health, auto, and home, at a minimum). And of course, your financial plan should also include provisions for a reasonable cash cushion (think of it as a "rainy day" fund) as well as a sensible retirement strategy.

If all this planning seems like a considerable amount of work, take a moment to consider the alternative. Without a plan to guide you, you'll be far more likely to squander your resources, including a most precious resource: your time. So, if you haven't already done so, take this opportunity to formulate a written financial plan for you and your family. And then, when you've committed yourself to a common-sense financial strategy, you're ready to create the indispensable tool for implementing your plan; that tool is your household budget.

Put Your Plan in Writing: It may take a few hours to commit your financial plans to paper, but it's most certainly worth the time and effort. Putting your plan down in black and white helps you clarify your thoughts, focus your energies, and measure your results.

Knowledge is only potential power. It becomes power only when and if it is organized into definite plans of actions and directed to a definite end.

Napoleon Hill

Are you disappointed, discouraged, and discontented with your present level of success? Are you secretly dissatisfied with your present status? Do you want to become a better and more beautiful person than you are today? Would you like to be able to really learn how to be proud of yourself and still not lose genuine humility? Then start dreaming! It's possible! You can become the person you have always wanted to be!

Robert Schuller

Too many people put their dreams "on hold." It takes an uncommon amount of guts to put your dreams on the line, to hold them up and say, "How good or bad am I?" That's where the courage comes in.

Erma Bombeck

Don't let the world define success for you. Only God can do that.

Jim Gallery

For this very reason, make every effort to supplement your faith with goodness, goodness with knowledge, knowledge with self-control, self-control with endurance, endurance with godliness.

2 Peter 1:5-6 HCSB

Wisdom is the principal thing; therefore get wisdom. And in all your getting, get understanding.

Proverbs 4:7 NKJV

Who is wise and understanding among you? Let him show by good conduct that his works are done in the meekness of wisdom.

James 3:13 NKJV

Now if any of you lacks wisdom, he should ask God, who gives to all generously and without criticizing, and it will be given to him.

James 1:5 HCSB

A wise man will listen and increase his learning, and a discerning man will obtain guidance.

Proverbs 1:5 HCSB

The fear of the Lord is the beginning of wisdom, and the knowledge of the Holy One is understanding.

Proverbs 9:10 NKJV

10 Common-Sense Ideas
About Investing Your Money

1. **Have an Investment Plan:** If you don't know where you want to go, you'll probably never get there.

2. **Diversify:** Mutual funds are an excellent way to diversify your stock holdings, but you shouldn't invest all of your investment dollars in mutual funds; you should be diversified, even in your diversity.

3. **Understand Your Investments:** You've got a good head on your shoulders; use it.

4. **Pay Attention to Your Investments, but Not Too Much Attention:** Keep an eye on your passive investments, but don't waste hours upon hours in front of the TV watching the daily twists and turns of the stock market; for the average investor, excessive market watching is a poor use of time and a distraction from more useful activities.

5. **Invest Consistently:** Once you begin an investment program, stick with it through good markets and bad ones.

6. **Don't Follow the Herd, Buy on the Bubble, or Attempt to Get Rich Quick:** The herd mentality leads to economic bubbles. Economic bubbles lead to excessive greed. Excessive greed leads to unwelcome losses. Investors beware: Those who attempt to get rich quick usually get poor instead.

7. **Invest in Businesses That Make Money Today, Not in Those That Hope to Make Money Some Day:** Whether you're investing in mutual funds or in interest-bearing instruments, make certain that your dollars are used to purchase investments in proven companies (or governmental entities) that produce recurring cash flow.

8. **Understand the Principle of Compound Interest:** The term "compound interest" means reinvesting interest earnings so that the interest itself begins to earn interest. This phenomenon, also referred to as "compounding," has profound implications for your financial future if you're patient enough to let your savings grow. Study the power of compound interest and put that power to work for you.

9. **Understand the Need for Adequate Liquidity:** The term "liquidity" refers to speed with which an investment can be sold for cash. Certain investments, such as publicly traded stocks and bonds, have a high level of liquidity. Other investments (such as real estate, collectibles, or stock in small businesses) have markedly less liquidity. As a general rule, the less liquidity an investment has, the more control you should be able to exercise over it.

10. **While You're Investing, Invest in Yourself, Too:** Your most important financial investments are the time, energy, and money that you use to improve your own professional skills. Never stop investing in yourself or in the tools of your trade.

Know What You Intend to Spend by Making a Budget

The plans of the diligent certainly lead to profit,
but anyone who is reckless only becomes poor.
Proverbs 21:5 HCSB

Do you have a written budget that tells you precisely where your money goes? If so, you've already taken an important step toward financial security. But if you don't have a budget, or if your budget is woefully out of date, please put down this book right now and begin writing the first draft of your new, improved, monthly household budget.

Far too many people "never quite get around" to making a budget. Why? Oftentimes, it's because these folks are afraid of the things that their budgets might reveal. Members of the non-budget crowd tell themselves that they're simply "too busy to budget" or that they're "bad with numbers." But in truth, these people are worried that their budgets might contain bad news; they're fearful that the cold hard facts may be too cold and too hard to take. But when it comes to money matters, ignorance is never bliss.

If you've been putting off the job of formulating your household budget, ask yourself why. And then, after that long embarrassing pause while you struggle, unsuccessfully, for a logical answer, start the budgeting process . . . now!

Creating a budget is relatively easy. Living by that budget can be considerably harder because life on a budget demands discipline and self-sacrifice. If you find yourself struggling to live within your means, perhaps you need a significantly larger dose of wisdom from the ultimate guidebook on disciplined living: the Holy Bible.

The Bible is God's Holy Word; it is intended, first and foremost, as a tool for communicating God's plan of salvation to mankind. Nevertheless, the Bible can teach you how to become a more disciplined person. And, as you become disciplined in other aspects of your life, you will also become more disciplined in the management of your personal finances.

God's Word is clear: as a believer, you are called to lead a life of moderation, maturity, and discipline. But the world often temps you to behave otherwise. Everywhere you turn, you will encounter powerful temptations to behave in undisciplined, intemperate, ungodly ways. And because you live in a world that glorifies material possessions, you will be tempted to squander your hard-earned money on a wide range of unnecessary purchases. Don't do it. Instead of spending now and worrying about it later, make a budget that makes sense. And live by it. When you do, you'll spend less time worrying and more time celebrating. And that, by the way, is precisely what God wants you to do.

If You're Not Saving Money, Your Budget Isn't Working:
All too often, our written budgets contain too much hope and too little reality. It's easy to deceive ourselves with budgets that don't reflect the reality of our particular situations. If you have a budget that reflects positive cash flow but a bank account that contains little or no cash, it's time for a reality check.

Budgeting is telling your money where to go instead of asking it where it went.

John Maxwell

Plan your work and your life. Without a system, you'll feel swamped.

Norman Vincent Peale

By failing to prepare, you are preparing to fail.

Ben Franklin

Success and happiness are not destinations. They are exciting, never-ending journeys.

Zig Ziglar

If your income is variable, budget and spend conservatively. For example, if your income depends heavily upon sales commissions, bonuses, overtime, or profit sharing, don't assume that next year will be as good as last year. The more your income changes, the more conservative you should be with your spending habits. And never spend variable income until the check has cleared.

But a noble person plans noble things . . . .

Isaiah 32:8 HCSB

A sensible person sees danger and takes cover, but the inexperienced keep going and are punished.

Proverbs 22:3 HCSB

Plans fail when there is no counsel, but with many advisers they succeed.

Proverbs 15:22 HCSB

Incline your ear to wisdom, and apply your heart to understanding.

Proverbs 2:2 NKJV

The wise store up knowledge, but the mouth of the fool hastens destruction.

Proverbs 10:14 HCSB

Give instruction to a wise man, and he will be still wiser; teach a just man, and he will increase in learning.

Proverbs 9:9 NKJV

If you don't know
where you're going, be careful.
You might get there.

—

Yogi Berra

Budgeting Basics

- Your budget should be realistic.

- You should write your budget down on paper, or if you're computer savvy, you may wish to use money-management software to organize your finances.

- Your budget should take into account all your major and minor expenses.

- If you're married, you should create your budget in cooperation with your spouse.

- You should leave room in your budget for surprises, and you should expect them.

- You should review your budget every month and compare it to your actual results.

- You should strive to live at a profit every month. If your budget reflects more expenses than income, you must find ways to cut your expenses or increase your income, or both. And in the meantime, you must cut your expenses to the minimum.

Sample Monthly Budget

Use the following budget as a guideline. Your monthly budget may be slightly different from this one, but it will probably contain most of the following elements:

Income

Monthly Income #1 (After Tax) = _____

Monthly Income #2 (After Tax) = _____

Interest Income (After Tax) = _____

Other Income (After Tax) = _____

Total Est. Income after Tax = _____

Expenses

Tithing = _____

Monthly Housing Expenses:

Rent/Mortgage Payment = _____

Association Fees = _____

Property Taxes = _____

Homeowner's Insurance = _____

Utilities

    Gas = _____

    Water = _____

    Electric = _____

    Trash Pickup = _____

Home Phone = _____

Cell Phone = _____

Cable TV = _____

Internet = _____

Misc. Home Maintenance = _____

Monthly Car Expenses:

Car Payments = _____

Auto Insurance = _____

Gasoline (Automobile) = _____

Regular Auto Service = _____

Misc. Auto Expenses = _____

Monthly Health Costs and Other Insurance:

Health Insurance = _____

Medicine = _____

Estimated Deductibles = _____

Donations = _____

Life Insurance = _____

Disability Insurance = _____

Other Insurance = _____

Other Monthly Expenses:

Household Supplies = _____

Groceries = _____

School Supplies = _____

Clothing = _____

Entertainment = _____

Travel = _____

Installment Loans = _____

Credit Card Payments = _____

Misc. Out-of-Pocket Expenses = _____

Total Est. Monthly Expenses = _____

Estimated Income After Expenses = _____

Notes to Yourself About Your Financial Plan

_____

_____

_____

_____

_____

_____

_____

_____

_____

_____

_____

_____

_____

_____

_____

_____

_____

_____

Principle 4

Live Within
Your Budget

Discipline yourself for the purpose of godliness.
1 Timothy 4:7 NASB

Y ou've probably heard this advice on thousands of occasions: "Spend less than you make." It sounds so easy, but it can be so hard. After all, we live in a world that is filled to the brim with wonderful things to buy and wonderful people telling us that we need to buy those things. But sometimes, our desires for more and better stuff can overload our ability to pay for the things we want. That's when Old Man Trouble arrives at the door.

The answer to the problem of overspending is straightforward. What's required is discipline. First, we must earn money through honest work for which we are well suited; then, we must spend less than we earn (and save the rest intelligently). This strategy of earning and saving money is simple to understand but much harder to put into practice. Thankfully, God gives clear instructions that, when followed, can lead us on the proper path.

> **Include Your Spouse:** Your household budget should ensure that your family (unlike many families) lives at a profit. And if you're married, be sure to include your spouse in the budgeting process.

God's Word reminds us again and again that our Creator expects us to lead disciplined lives. God doesn't reward laziness, misbehavior, or apathy. To the contrary, He expects us to behave with dignity and discipline. But ours is a world in which dignity and discipline are often in short supply.

We live in a world in which leisure is glorified and indifference is often glamorized. But God has other plans. God gives us talents, and He expects us to use them. Of course, it is seldom easy to cultivate those talents. Sometimes, we must invest countless hours (or, in some cases, many years) honing our skills. And that's perfectly okay with God, because He understands that self-discipline is a blessing, not a burden.

Proverbs 23:12 advises: "Apply your heart to discipline And your ears to words of knowledge" (NASB). And, 2 Peter 1:5-6 teaches, "make every effort to supplement your faith with goodness, goodness with knowledge, knowledge with self-control, self-control with endurance, endurance with godliness" (Holman CSB). Thus, God's Word is clear: we must exercise self-discipline in all matters, including our finances.

When we pause to consider how much work needs to be done, we realize that self-discipline is not simply a proven way to get ahead; it's also an integral part of God's plan for our lives. If we genuinely seek to be faithful stewards of our time, our talents, and our resources, we must adopt a disciplined approach to life. There's simply no other way.

Discipline is the basic set of tools we require to solve life's problems.

M. Scott Peck

Work is doing it. Discipline is doing it every day. Diligence is doing it well every day.

Dave Ramsey

"They that sow bountifully shall reap also bountifully," is as true in spiritual things as in material.

Lottie Moon

Personal humility is a spiritual discipline and the hallmark of the service of Jesus.

Franklin Graham

As we make an offering of our work, we find the truth of a principle Jesus taught: Fulfillment is not a goal to achieve, but always the by-product of a sacrifice.

Elisabeth Elliot

Working in the vineyard, Working all the day, Never be discouraged, Only watch and pray.

Fanny Crosby

No discipline seems enjoyable at the time, but painful. Later on, however, it yields the fruit of peace and righteousness to those who have been trained by it.

Hebrews 12:11 HCSB

The one who follows instruction is on the path to life, but the one who rejects correction goes astray.

Proverbs 10:17 HCSB

For this very reason, make every effort to supplement your faith with goodness, goodness with knowledge, knowledge with self-control, self-control with endurance, endurance with godliness.

2 Peter 1:5-6 HCSB

I discipline my body and bring it under strict control, so that after preaching to others, I myself will not be disqualified.

1 Corinthians 9:27 HCSB

Therefore by their fruits you will know them.

Matthew 7:20 NKJV

Common-Sense Tips
for Saving Money

- **Plan Ahead:** If you wait till the last minute, you invariably pay more. But, if you plan ahead, you can shop at the most affordable stores and you can buy things on sale.

- **Generic? Absolutely!** Today, almost every retail product has its generic equivalent. Often, these generic products are almost identical to higher priced brand name products. Do yourself a favor and check out the generic equivalents of the products you buy.

- **More Convenience Usually Costs More:** When you drop in and buy a bag of chips at the local convenience store, you'll often pay twice as much as you would at the local grocery store. Think about it.

- **Coupons?** Clipping coupons is a great way to save money if you only clip coupons for the items that you really need.

- **Off-season Purchases Save Money:** The best time to buy a bathing suit is in September, and the best time to buy a winter coat is in February.

- **Today's Amazing Cost-Cutting World:** In addition to wholesale clubs, there are a wide range of low-cost alternatives to traditional retailers. If you snoop around, you'll probably find stores in your community that sell all sorts of things at reduced prices. Check them out.

- **Understand the Bills You Pay:** We live in a world where every company, or so it seems, is "fee happy." And all those little fees can add up. When you receive a bill, especially one from a big company, watch for "transaction fees," "access fees," "roaming charges," "user fees," "prep fees," or any charge that ends with the word "pass-through." If you can't have the fee waived, you may want to consider changing to another vendor.

- **Wholesale Clubs? Yes, But . . .** Wholesale clubs are wonderful if you use them often enough to justify their annual fees. And if you decide to join a wholesale club, check out all its services, including insurance, long distance phone cards, and automotive products, to name but a few.

Make the Choice to Live at a Profit

*Don't collect for yourselves treasures on earth,
where moth and rust destroy and where thieves break in
and steal. But collect for yourselves treasures in heaven,
where neither moth nor rust destroys,
and where thieves don't break in and steal.
For where your treasure is, there your heart will be also.*
Matthew 6:19-21 HCSB

Spending money is an incredibly easy thing to do. After all, the shopping malls and discount stores are filled to the ceilings with attractively packaged items, all of which were created for a single purpose: so that we, the consuming public, might buy them.

But when we spend more than we should—when we become overly absorbed with the acquisition of things—complications arise. Each new acquisition costs money or time, and often both. To further complicate matters, many items can be purchased, not with real money, but with something much more insidious: debt. Debt—especially consumer debt used to purchase items that immediately go down in value—is a modern-day form of indentured servitude.

If you're looking for a sure-fire, time-tested way to simplify your life and thereby improve your world, learn to control your possessions before they control you. Purchase only those things that make a significant contribution to your well being and the well being of your family. Never spend more than you make. Understand the folly in buying consumer goods on credit. Never use credit cards as a way of financing your lifestyle.

Ask yourself this simple question: "Do I own my possessions, or do they own me?" If you don't like the answer you receive, make an ironclad promise to stop acquiring and start divesting. Make up your mind to live at a profit, even if that means making radical changes in the way you spend money.

When you begin spending less, you'll be amazed at the things you can do without. You'll be pleasantly surprised at the sense of satisfaction that accompanies your newfound moderation. And you'll understand firsthand that when it comes to material possessions, less truly is more.

When You Finance Your Purchase, You Pay More: All other things being equal, you will usually pay more when you purchase items on credit. If you want the best price for an item, whether it's a new car, a new suit, or a new house, bring cash and be willing to negotiate with the seller. If you want to pay more, bring no cash and be willing to accept the seller's terms.

TWO-QUESTION POP QUIZ:

1. How much money should you be saving each month?

2. How much money are you actually saving each month?

No test of a man's true character is more conclusive than how he spends his time and his money.

Patrick Morley

Have you prayed about your resources lately? Find out how God wants you to use your time and your money. No matter what it costs, forsake all that is not of God.

Kay Arthur

If a person gets his attitude toward money straight, it will help straighten out almost every other area of his life.

Billy Graham

Money is a mirror that, strange as it sounds, reflects our personal weaknesses and strengths with amazing clarity.

Dave Ramsey

There is nothing wrong with people possessing riches. The wrong comes when riches possess people.

Billy Graham

The one who loves money is never satisfied with money, and whoever loves wealth [is] never [satisfied] with income. This too is futile.

Ecclesiastes 5:10 HCSB

No servant can be the slave of two masters, since either he will hate one and love the other, or he will be devoted to one and despise the other. You can't be slaves to both God and money.

Luke 16:13 HCSB

A faithful man shall abound with blessings: but he that maketh haste to be rich shall not be innocent.

Proverbs 28:20 KJV

If riches increase, set not your heart upon them.

Psalm 62:10 KJV

And Jesus went into the temple of God, and cast out all them that sold and bought in the temple, and overthrew the tables of the money changers, and the seats of them that sold doves, and said unto them, It is written, My house shall be called the house of prayer; but ye have made it a den of thieves.

Matthew 21:12-13 KJV

Your life should be free from the love of money. Be satisfied with what you have, for He Himself has said, I will never leave you or forsake you.

Hebrews 13:5 HCSB

Teaching Your Children
to Manage Money

If you're a parent, you don't need anybody to tell you the obvious: Your child is a priceless gift from the Father above. You also know, from firsthand experience, that the job of parenting is an immense responsibility.

One of your parental duties is to teach your child how to manage money. The following ideas can help:

"And the Greatest of These Is Love . . ." When it comes to the art of raising children, 1 Corinthians 13:13 certainly applies: The "greatest of these" is, indeed, love. Every child deserves to grow up in a safe, loving, God-fearing home, and it's up to you to make certain that your home fits that description.

Teach by Example: As you begin to teach your child a few common-sense principles about managing money, your actions will speak far more loudly than your words. Parental pronouncements are easy to make but much harder to live by. As a parent, you are not just a role model; you are the role model. Behave accordingly.

The World Won't Protect Your Child from the Consequences of Frivolous Spending, and neither should you.

As a parent, your job is to ensure that the consequences of your child's actions are logical, measured, appropriate, and thoroughly understood by your youngster.

Share Your Ideas and Your Faith: You need not have attended seminary (or, for that matter, business school) to have worthwhile opinions about faith and finances. Express those opinions clearly and consistently. Your kids need to know where you stand.

You live in a highly complicated world that is definitely not designed to help you achieve financial independence. To the contrary, most of the messages you hear and see each day are intended to induce you to spend money, not to save it. But, in order to have money, you must learn not only how to earn it, you must also learn how to keep it. And, as we all know, keeping money is often harder than earning it. So if you're having trouble saving money, take a careful look at your spending habits. When you do, you'll probably discover that you're buying lots of things that you don't really need.

Identifying Your Biggest
Budget-Busters

On the lines below, identify the sorts of expenses that most often prevent you from living within your budget. Then, after you've identified your most likely budget-busting cost overruns, think carefully—and prayerfully—about steps you can take to ensure that, in the future, you stick tenaciously to your budget.

_____

_____

_____

_____

_____

_____

_____

_____

_____

_____

_____

_____

Notes to Yourself About Your Spending Habits

On the lines below, take a moment to assess your spending habits. Give yourself a grade from A to F. If necessary, take time to identify frivolous expenditures or impulse purchases that you should avoid in the future.

_____

_____

_____

_____

_____

_____

_____

_____

_____

_____

_____

_____

_____

Principle 5

Avoid Debt

The borrower is a slave to the lender.
Proverbs 22:7 HCSB

We live in a world that has become so reliant upon debt that our entire economy depends upon it. How many new automobiles would dealers sell if there were no car loans? Not very many. And how many businesses would cease operations if their short-term credit lines were "called" tomorrow? Plenty! Face it: we live in a world that is addicted to debt, but you needn't be. Just because our world revolves around borrowed money doesn't mean that you must do likewise.

Of course, not all debt is dangerous to your financial health. If you borrow money to purchase a well-located home—if you make a sensible down payment, and if you can comfortably afford all the expenses of owning and maintaining your residence—then you're probably making a wise decision by becoming a homeowner. Why? Because home mortgage debt, when used judiciously, can have a positive influence on your financial well-being. But other forms of debt are not so benign.

If you're already living beyond your means and borrowing to pay for the privilege, then you know that sleepless nights and stress-filled days are the psychological payments that must be extracted from those who buy too much "now" in hopes that they can pay for those things "later." Unfortunately, "later" usually arrives sooner than expected, and that's when the trouble begins.

Everywhere you turn, businesses are trying to convince you to become their debtor. Credit cards (which are advertised as "low-interest" but aren't) are easy to acquire, even easier to use, and, at times, incredibly difficult to pay off. In fact, excessive credit card debt has brought untold misery to countless families, and it's your job to ensure that your family is spared from this needless suffering.

Sometimes, you don't need a credit card to get yourself into trouble. Offers of "zero-down" or "zero-percent financing," which are designed to let you spend less now while spending more in the long run, are dangerous to your financial health. When the financing looks too good to be true, it probably is. In almost every case, you're better off paying cash.

Whether you're buying a mattress, a microwave, or a Maserati, somebody will probably be willing to sell it to you on credit. But the Bible makes it clear that the instant you become a debtor, you also become a servant to the lender (Proverbs 22:7). So do yourself and your family a favor by taking the following simple steps:

1. Pay your credit card balances off every month. If you can't manage to pay off all your balances when they come due, put your credit cards in a drawer and don't use them again until you've paid them off completely.

2. Never buy consumer goods such as clothes, furniture, or electronics on credit. Even if the interest rate seems incredibly attractive, don't sign your name on the dotted line; wait until you can afford to pay cash.

3. Don't rent consumer goods or electronics on "rent-to-own" plans. These plans may sound good, but they aren't.

4. If you absolutely must borrow money to purchase a car, buy a good, safe, inexpensive used car that you can pay off in a hurry. It's better to drive a clunker with a small note than a luxury car that's "loaded" with debt.

To sum it up, debt has a few good uses and many bad ones. So beware. And if you're trying to decide whether or not to make that next big purchase, remember that when it comes to borrowed money, less is usually more . . . much more.

A Mortgage on Your Home Is Okay . . . Within Reason:
Unless you were born with a substantial trust fund—and
if you were, you're probably not reading this book—you
will need to borrow money to purchase your home.
And, because home ownership has many benefits, you're
probably wise to do so if you use common sense. Don't
try to "max out" your mortgage by borrowing every
penny that you can. And don't load yourself down with
a second mortgage that can further crimp your financial
style. Instead, wait until you have saved enough money to
make a substantial down payment, and don't buy a more
expensive home than you can afford.

Simple Rules About
Borrowing Money

1. Since the borrower is servant to the lender, don't ever borrow money without giving it very careful (and prayerful) consideration.

2. Don't borrow money to buy consumer goods that will inevitably go down in value.

3. When you borrow money to purchase a home, be conservative.

4. If you're thinking about co-signing someone else's note, remember that once you sign your name to the dotted line, your liability is real, very real indeed. So, if you are about to co-sign someone else's obligation, follow this simple advice: don't do it.

When you follow these guidelines, you'll not only improve your financial fitness; you'll also sleep better at night.

Getting out of the pit requires we surround ourselves with people who love us enough to support us and lift us up when we are at our ugliest.

Dave Ramsey

Having money may not make people happy, but owing money is sure to make them miserable.

John Maxwell

God says that when you borrow, you become a servant of the lender; the lender is established as an authority over the borrower. (Proverbs 22:7)

Larry Burkett

It is better to go to bed supperless than rise in debt.

Ben Franklin

Debt is like any other trap. It is easy enough to get into but hard enough to get out of.

Josh Billings

Credit Cards 101:

Don't Use Credit Cards to Finance Your Lifestyle: Credit cards should never be confused with banks. If you want a business loan for a legitimate purpose, go to a lending institution. If you need a mortgage on your home, call a reputable broker. But if you're about to buy a consumable item on credit, be sure that you can pay for it when the bill comes due.

Credit Cards 201:

How to Tell If You're Not Using Your Credit Cards Wisely: If your credit card balance is more than you can comfortably pay each time the bill comes due, then you're charging too much.

Learn from Your Mistakes

The one who conceals his sins will not prosper,
but whoever confesses and renounces
them will find mercy.
Proverbs 28:13 HCSB

Are you one of those people who has, at one time or another, made a mess of your financial affairs? If so, welcome to a very large club! Almost everyone experiences financial pressures from time to time, and so, perhaps, will you.

Winston Churchill once observed, "Success is going from failure to failure without loss of enthusiasm." What was good for Churchill is also good for you, too. As you live and learn about life, you should expect to make mistakes—and a few financial blunders, too—but you should not allow those missteps to rob you of the enthusiasm you need to fulfill God's plan for your life.

We are imperfect people living in an imperfect world; mistakes are simply part of the price we pay for being here. But, even though mistakes are an inevitable part of life's journey, repeated mistakes should not be. When we commit the inevitable missteps of life, we must correct them, learn from them, and pray for the wisdom not to repeat them.

When we do, our mistakes become lessons, and our lives become adventures in growth, not stagnation.

Have you made a financial foul-up or two? You probably have. But here's the big question: Have you used your mistakes as stumbling blocks or stepping stones? The answer to that question will determine how quickly you gain financial security and peace of mind.

In Times of Financial Hardship . . .

All families endure times of sadness, disappointment, or hardship. If your troubles seem overwhelming, be willing to seek outside help—starting, of course, with your pastor.

Take Responsibility for Your Financial Condition. If your finances are in a mess, prayerfully ask God to help you become a better steward of the resources He has entrusted to you.

Very few things motivate us to give God our undivided attention like being faced with the negative consequences of our decisions.

Charles Stanley

It's your choice: you can either count your blessings or recount your disappointments.

Jim Gallery

Failure is one of life's most powerful teachers. How we handle our failures determines whether we're going to simply "get by" in life or "press on."

Beth Moore

Mistakes offer the possibility for redemption and a new start in God's kingdom. No matter what you're guilty of, God can restore your innocence.

Barbara Johnson

Father, take our mistakes and turn them into opportunities.

Max Lucado

If we confess our sins to him, he is faithful and just to forgive us and to cleanse us from every wrong.

1 John 1:9 NLT

If you listen to constructive criticism, you will be at home among the wise.

Proverbs 15:31 NLT

The one who walks with the wise will become wise, but a companion of fools will suffer harm.

Proverbs 13:20 HCSB

For a righteous man may fall seven times and rise again.

Proverbs 24:16 NKJV

Do not remember the past events, pay no attention to things of old. Look, I am about to do something new; even now it is coming. Do you not see it? Indeed, I will make a way in the wilderness, rivers in the desert.

Isaiah 43:18-19 HCSB

Starting Over

Sometimes our losses mean that we must start over. From scratch. As believers we can find comfort in the knowledge that wherever we find ourselves, whether on the mountaintops of life or in the deepest valleys of despair, God is there with us.

Do not lose courage in considering your own imperfections.

—

St. Francis of Sales

Are You Comfortable with Your Obligations?

On the lines below, make notes to yourself about your current level of debt. Do you wish you owed less? Are you trying to decrease debt without much success? If so, jot down at least three steps that you can take today to begin paying off your obligations more quickly.

_____

_____

_____

_____

_____

_____

_____

_____

_____

_____

_____

Principle 6

Build Up Your Reserves

The wise have wealth and luxury,
but fools spend whatever they get.
Proverbs 21:20 NLT

Far too many people live from paycheck to paycheck with almost no cash reserves to use in case of emergencies. But you don't have to live that way, and you shouldn't. Instead of spending your entire paycheck, you should establish the habit of saving money every month, even if doing so requires a dramatic modification in your spending habits.

How big of a nest egg should you keep in reserve? It depends upon your circumstances. If you have stable employment, if you're living at a profit, if you're not overly burdened by debt, and if you're a two-income family, then you can probably feel comfortable by keeping four to six month's living expenses in cash (or cash-equivalent assets like certificates of deposit). But, if your income is less predictable, or if that income might be more difficult to replace in the event you lose your job, then you should probably strive to keep enough cash to support you and your family for up to a year. This emergency fund should be kept in federally insured, readily available, interest-bearing accounts.

What should you do if you don't have any cash reserves now? Well first, you should work to pay off any short-term, high-interest debts (like credit card balances), and then, once you're debt-free (except for your home mortgage), you should begin socking away money from every paycheck until you meet and exceed your comfort level.

When you establish a sensible emergency fund, you'll sleep better at night . . . and you'll be ready if the unexpected happens.

The Best Things in Life Seldom Happen Overnight: They usually take time. Henry Blackaby writes, "The grass that is here today and gone tomorrow does not require much time to mature. A big oak tree that lasts for generations requires much more time to grow and mature. God is concerned about your life through eternity. Allow Him to take all the time He needs to shape you for His purposes. Larger assignments will require longer periods of preparation." And those words apply not only to spiritual maturity, but also to financial security. So if you're intent upon building a sizeable monetary nest egg, be patient . . . very patient.

Invest and Keep Investing

It is better to have self-control than to conquer a city.
Proverbs 16:32 NLT

If you want your investments to grow, you should establish a budget that allows you to save money from every paycheck. And you should stick to that budget. After all, you can't build a meaningful nest egg if you're living beyond your means. Yet you inhabit a world that is designed to empty your wallet as soon as possible, if not sooner. Your job is to live within your budget and to avoid impulse purchases, especially big impulse purchases.

When you invest wisely, and when you allow your investments to grow for years at a time without making periodic withdrawals for unnecessary expenses, you'll watch your nest egg grow and grow. But if you're one of those people who insists upon buying some new toy every time the savings account hits five digits, you'll end up with a house full of worn-out toys but very little savings.

So here's a tip: when it comes to any investment plan, consistency is the key. That means you'll need to save and keep saving every month. No exceptions.

Self-discipline Every Day: A self-disciplined lifestyle requires consistency. And if you want to enjoy the financial security that belongs to those who adopt a disciplined approach to life, then you must learn to control yourself seven days a week.

But as for you, be strong;
don't be discouraged,
for your work has a reward.

—

2 Chronicles 15:7 HCSB

Do you not know that the runners in a stadium all race, but only one receives the prize? Run in such a way that you may win. Now everyone who competes exercises self-control in everything. However, they do it to receive a perishable crown, but we an imperishable one.

1 Corinthians 9:24-25 HCSB

I have fought the good fight, I have finished the race, I have kept the faith.

2 Timothy 4:7 HCSB

So we must not get tired of doing good, for we will reap at the proper time if we don't give up.

Galatians 6:9 HCSB

Let us lay aside every weight and the sin that so easily ensnares us, and run with endurance the race that lies before us, keeping our eyes on Jesus, the source and perfecter of our faith.

Hebrews 12:1-2 HCSB

Now we want each of you to demonstrate the same diligence for the final realization of your hope, so that you won't become lazy, but imitators of those who inherit the promises through faith and perseverance.

Hebrews 6:11-12 HCSB

Keep adding, keep walking, keep advancing; do not stop, do not turn back, do not turn from the straight road.

St. Augustine

In the Bible, patience is not a passive acceptance of circumstances. It is a courageous perseverance in the face of suffering and difficulty.

Warren Wiersbe

Battles are won in the trenches, in the grit and grime of courageous determination; they are won day by day in the arena of life.

Charles Swindoll

Courage and perseverance have a magical talisman, before which difficulties disappear and obstacles vanish into thin air.

John Quincy Adams

Patience and diligence, like faith, move mountains.

William Penn

Perseverance is more than endurance. It is endurance combined with absolute assurance and certainty that what we are looking for is going to happen.

Oswald Chambers

Notes to Yourself
About Your Financial Reserves

On the lines below, make notes to yourself concerning the amount of cash you need to keep in your rainy-day reserve account. Take into consideration factors such as the predictability of your income, the needs of your family, and the current state of your finances.

_____

_____

_____

_____

_____

_____

_____

_____

_____

_____

Principle 7

Find Work You Can Be Passionate About

Whatever you do, do it enthusiastically,
as something done for the Lord and not for men.
Colossians 3:23 HCSB

If you've found work that you love, and if, through your efforts, you help make the world a better place, consider yourself doubly blessed. But, if you're dissatisfied with your employment, or if you feel that your professional life is not pleasing to God, then there's only one thing to do: you must keep searching.

Perhaps you've been searching for work that is pleasing to other people. Or perhaps you find yourself struggling in a job that is not suited to your skills. In either case, you must remember that God made you exactly as you are, and He did so for a very good reason: His reason. Therefore, you must glorify God by honoring the talents that He gave you, not the talents that you wish He had given you.

When you discover the work for which God created you, you'll be productive and inspired. But until you find that work, you'll have trouble generating enthusiasm. Unfortunately, too many of us have become intensely passionate about the things that improve neither the world nor ourselves. We may fritter away precious hours in front of the television. Or we may fall deeply in love with alcohol, drugs, gambling, or other addictive behaviors that leave little time or energy for anything else.

> We must trust as if it all depended on God and work as if it all depended on us.
> C. H. Spurgeon

Have you found work about which you are passionate? Have you discovered a vocation that inspires you to arrive at the office ten minutes early rather than ten minutes late? Does your work help to create a better world and a better you? If the answer to these questions is yes, then consider yourself both fortunate and wise. But if the dream of meaningful work remains elusive, keep searching—and praying—until you find it.

Feeling a little lazy?

That means that you're not excited about your work. So here's your challenge: find work that's so much fun you can't wait to clock in. When you do, you'll discover that a really good job beats leisure (or retirement) hands down.

In the long run, it makes little difference how cleverly others are deceived; if we are not doing what we are best equipped to do, there will be a core of unhappiness in our lives which will be more and more difficult to ignore as the years pass.

Dorothea Brande

You usually enjoy what you're good at.

Cal Turner, Sr.

God provides the ingredients for our daily bread but expects us to do the baking. With our own hands!

Barbara Johnson

The world does not consider labor a blessing, therefore it flees and hates it, but the pious who fear the Lord labor with a ready and cheerful heart, for they know God's command, and they acknowledge His calling.

Martin Luther

If, in your working hours, you make the work your end, you will presently find yourself all unawares inside the only circle in your profession that really matters. You will be one of the sound craftsmen, and other sound craftsmen will know it.

C. S. Lewis

Whatever your hands find to do, do with [all] your strength.

Ecclesiastes 9:10 HCSB

He did it with all his heart. So he prospered.

2 Chronicles 31:21 NKJV

Don't work only while being watched, in order to please men, but as slaves of Christ, do God's will from your heart. Render service with a good attitude, as to the Lord and not to men.

Ephesians 6:6-7 HCSB

We must do the works of Him who sent Me while it is day. Night is coming when no one can work.

John 9:4 HCSB

Lazy people's desire for sleep will kill them, because they refuse to work. All day long they wish for more, but good people give without holding back.

Proverbs 21:25-26 NKJV

Be strong and courageous, and do the work.

1 Chronicles 28:20 HCSB

Maximize the Talents God Has Given You

Do not neglect the gift that is in you.
1 Timothy 4:14 HCSB

An important element in achieving financial security is learning what to do with the talents God has given you. All of us have special talents and unique opportunities—you are no exception. But your talent is no guarantee of success; it must be cultivated and nurtured; otherwise, it will go unused . . . and God's gift to you will be squandered.

In the 25th chapter of Matthew, Jesus tells the "Parable of the Talents." In it, He describes a master who leaves his servants with varying amounts of money (talents). When the master returns, some servants have put their money to work and earned more, to which the master responds, "Well done, good and faithful servant! You have been faithful with a few things; I will put you in charge of many things. Come and share your master's happiness!" (Matthew 25:21 NIV)

But the story does not end so happily for the foolish servant

> You are the only person on earth who can use your ability.
> Zig Ziglar

who was given a single talent but did nothing with it. For this man, the master has nothing but reproach: "You wicked, lazy servant . . ." (Matthew 25:26 NIV). The message from Jesus is clear: We must use our talents, not waste them.

Your particular talent is a treasure on temporary loan from God. He intends for your talent to enrich the world and enrich your life. Value the gift that God has given you, nourish it, make it grow, and share it with the world. Then, when you meet your Master face-to-face, you, too, will hear those wonderful words, "Well done, good and faithful servant! . . . Come and share your Master's happiness!" And until that glorious day arrives, you'll have the satisfaction of knowing that you've made the world a better place by using the talents and opportunities that are uniquely yours.

Invest in Your Own Earning Power

The world keeps changing, and so should you. Your current job may not last forever, so you'd best begin planning for the next one now. An investment in yourself pays powerful dividends.

Employ whatever God has entrusted you with, in doing good, all possible good, in every possible kind and degree.

John Wesley

God has given you special talents—now it's your turn to give them back to God.

Marie T. Freeman

If you want to reach your potential, you need to add a strong work ethic to your talent.

John Maxwell

Not everyone possesses boundless energy or a conspicuous talent. We are not equally blessed with great intellect or physical beauty or emotional strength. But we have all been given the same ability to be faithful.

Gigi Graham Tchividjian

God often reveals His direction for our lives through the way He made us . . . with a certain personality and unique skills.

Bill Hybels

Each one has his own gift from God, one in this manner and another in that.

1 Corinthians 7:7 NKJV

So he who had received five talents came and brought five other talents, saying, "Lord, you delivered to me five talents; look, I have gained five more talents besides them." His lord said to him, "Well done, good and faithful servant; you were faithful over a few things, I will make you ruler over many things. Enter into the joy of your lord."

Matthew 25:20-21 NKJV

Based on the gift they have received, everyone should use it to serve others, as good managers of the varied grace of God.

1 Peter 4:10 HCSB

According to the grace given to us, we have different gifts: If prophecy, use it according to the standard of faith; if service, in service; if teaching, in teaching; if exhorting, in exhortation; giving, with generosity; leading, with diligence; showing mercy, with cheerfulness.

Romans 12:6-8 HCSB

Every good gift and every perfect gift is from above, and cometh down from the Father of lights.

James 1:17 KJV

*I remind you to keep ablaze
the gift of God that is in you.*

—

2 Timothy 1:6 HCSB

In the good old days, you might go to work for a company, work there for thirty years, and retire with both a gold watch and a decent pension. But these aren't the good old days; they're the good new days, and the rules have changed.

Today, even if you're working for an established company, you cannot be sure that you'll be working there when you retire, even if you're the best employee in the history of capitalism! Why? In today's rapid-fire business environment, even the very best employees may be swept out on the tides of change. That's why today's perfect job may be tomorrow's fond memory. And that's why you'd best prepare yourself for the inevitable changes that are probably right around the corner.

Invest in Yourself

Investments in education and career development pay the biggest dividends. Make learning a lifelong endeavor.

Notes to Yourself

On the lines below write about the passion—or lack of passion—that you feel for your work; and where you feel your talents and your opportunities are and ways to maximize them.

_____

_____

_____

_____

_____

_____

_____

_____

_____

_____

_____

_____

Principle 8

Keep Money in Perspective

*For the love of money is a root of all kinds of evil,
for which some have strayed from the faith in their
greediness, and pierced themselves through with many
sorrows. But you, O man of God, flee these things and
pursue righteousness, godliness, faith,
love, patience, gentleness.*

1 Timothy 6:10-11 NKJV

The Bible clearly warns us that the love of money is "a root of all kinds of evil." So when we consider ways to save money and accumulate wealth, we must beware. Money, in and of itself, is not evil, but worshipping money is.

Are you placing too much priority on money? Are you more focused on your next paycheck than you are on God? Do you spend more time thinking about your next acquisition than you do about God's plan for your life? If so, it's time to talk seriously to God about your priorities.

Today, as you prioritize matters of importance for you and yours, remember that God is almighty, but the dollar is not. If we worship God, we are blessed. But if we worship "the almighty dollar," we are inevitably punished because of our misplaced priorities—and our punishment inevitably comes sooner rather than later.

Don't fall in love with "stuff."

We live in a society that worships "stuff"—don't fall into that trap. Remember this: "stuff" is highly overrated. Worship God almighty, not the almighty dollar. (Proverbs 11:28)

Greed is evil because it substitutes material things for the place of honor that the Creator ought to have in an individual's life.

Charles Stanley

Greed is enslaving. The more you have, the more you want—until eventually avarice consumes you.

Kay Arthur

Many things I have tried to grasp and have lost. That which I have placed in God's hands I still have.

Martin Luther

A person who hungers for money will starve to death spiritually!

Anonymous

Nothing is really ours until we share it.

C. S. Lewis

If a Christian is worried, frustrated, and upset about money, God is not in control.

Larry Burkett

Finding Peace

Sometimes, our financial struggles are simply manifestations of the inner conflict that we feel when we stray from God's path. The beautiful words of John 14:27 remind us that Jesus offers us peace, not as the world gives, but as He alone gives. Our challenge is to accept Christ's peace into our hearts and then, as best we can, to share His peace with our families and friends.

When we summon the courage and the determination to implement a sensible financial plan, we invite peace into our lives. But, we should never confuse earthly peace (with a small "p") with spiritual Peace (the heavenly Peace–with a capital "P"–that flows from the Prince of Peace).

When we accept Jesus as our personal Savior, we are transformed by His grace. We are then free to accept the spiritual abundance and peace that can be ours through the power of the risen Christ.

Have you found the genuine peace that can be yours through Christ? Or are you still rushing after the illusion of "peace and happiness" that the world promises but cannot deliver? Today, as a gift to yourself and to your loved ones, claim the inner peace that is your spiritual birthright: the peace of Jesus Christ. It is offered freely; it has been paid for in full; it is yours for the asking. So ask. And then share.

Financial peace can, and should, be yours. But the spiritual peace that stems from your personal relationship with Jesus must be yours if you are to receive the eternal abundance of our Lord. Claim that abundance today.

Peace I leave with you.
My peace I give to you.
I do not give to you as the world gives.
Your heart must not be
troubled or fearful.

—

John 14:27 HCSB

When in Doubt, Be More Generous Than Necessary

And let us not grow weary while doing good,
for in due season we shall reap if we do not lose heart.
Galatians 6:9 NKJV

The thread of generosity is woven—completely and inextricably—into the very fabric of Christ's teachings. As He sent His disciples out to heal the sick and spread God's message of salvation, Jesus offered this guiding principle: "Freely you have received, freely give" (Matthew 10:8 NIV). The principle still applies. If we are to be disciples of Christ, we must give freely of our time, our possessions, and our love.

In 2 Corinthians 9, Paul reminds us that when we sow the seeds of generosity, we reap bountiful rewards in accordance with God's plan for our lives. Thus, we are instructed to give cheerfully and without reservation: "But this I say, He which soweth sparingly shall reap also sparingly; and he which soweth bountifully shall reap also bountifully. Every man according as he purposeth in his heart, so let him give; not grudgingly, or of necessity: for God loveth a cheerful giver" (vv. 6-7 KJV).

One of the greatest joys of financial independence is the ability to share your financial blessings with others. The more you earn and save, the more you'll have to share. So today, make this pledge and keep it: Be a cheerful, generous, courageous giver. The world needs your help, and you need the spiritual rewards that will be yours when you do.

We hurt people by being too busy, too busy to notice their needs.

—

Billy Graham

Here's a scary thought: the content of your character is demonstrated by the way you choose to spend money. If you spend money wisely, and if you give God His fair share, then you're doing just fine. But if you're up to your eyeballs in debt, and if "shop till you drop" is your unofficial motto, it's time to retire the credit cards and rearrange your priorities.

Our society is in love with money and the things that money can buy. God is not. God cares about people, not possessions, and so must we. We must, to the best of our abilities, love our neighbors as ourselves, and we must, to the best of our abilities, resist the mighty temptation to place possessions ahead of people.

Money, in and of itself, is not evil; worshipping money is. So today, as you prioritize matters of importance for you and yours, remember that God is almighty, but the dollar is not.

Are you choosing to make money your master? If so, it's time to turn your thoughts and your prayers to more important matters. And, it's time to begin storing up riches that will endure throughout eternity: the spiritual kind.

It is one of the most beautiful compensations of life that no one can sincerely try to help another without helping herself.

Barbara Johnson

Make it a rule, and pray to God to help you to keep it, never, if possible, to lie down at night without being able to say: "I have made one human being at least a little wiser, or a little happier, or at least a little better this day."

Charles Kingsley

When you add value to others, you do not take anything away from yourself.

John Maxwell

Fragile and delicate are the feelings of most who seek our help. They need to sense we are there because we care . . . not just because it's our job.

Charles Swindoll

God does not supply money to satisfy our every whim and desire. His promise is to meet our needs and provide an abundance so that we can help other people.

Larry Burkett

If you really carry out the royal law prescribed in Scripture, You shall love your neighbor as yourself, you are doing well.

James 2:8 HCSB

As we have therefore opportunity, let us do good unto all men, especially unto them who are of the household of faith.

Galatians 6:10 KJV

In every way I've shown you that by laboring like this, it is necessary to help the weak and to keep in mind the words of the Lord Jesus, for He said, "It is more blessed to give than to receive."

Acts 20:35 HCSB

Let this mind be in you which was also in Christ Jesus, who . . . made Himself of no reputation, taking the form of a bondservant, and coming in the likeness of men.

Philippians 2:5,7 NKJV

The greatest among you will be your servant. Whoever exalts himself will be humbled, and whoever humbles himself will be exalted.

Matthew 23:11-12 HCSB

The one who has two shirts must share with someone who has none, and the one who has food must do the same.

Luke 3:11 HCSB

How Important Is Money to You?

In the space below, describe the importance you place upon money and the material possessions that money can buy. If you find that you're placing too much importance on money, think carefully about the role that money currently plays in your life—and the role that it should play. Then, jot down at least ten ways that you can be more generous.

_____

_____

_____

_____

_____

_____

_____

_____

_____

_____

Principle 9

Avoid the Trap of Materialism

And He told them, "Watch out and be on guard against all greed, because one's life is not in the abundance of his possessions."
Luke 12:15 HCSB

I n our modern society, we need money to live. But as Christians, we must never make the acquisition of money the central focus of our lives. Money is a tool, but it should never overwhelm our sensibilities. The focus of life must be squarely on things spiritual, not things material.

Whenever we place our love for material possessions above our love for God—or when we yield to the countless other temptations of everyday living—we find ourselves engaged in a struggle between good and evil. Let us respond to this struggle by freeing ourselves from that subtle yet powerful temptation: the temptation to love the world more than we love God.

Whenever we become absorbed with the acquisition of things, complications arise. Each new acquisition costs money or time, often both. To further complicate matters, many items can be purchased, not with real money, but with something much more insidious: debt. Debt—especially consumer debt used to purchase depreciating assets—is a modern-day form of indentured servitude. So do yourself and your family a favor: Pay as you go. In other words, don't buy stuff—especially expensive consumer items that quickly go down in value—unless you have the money to pay for them in your bank account.

Want a boat? Save up until you can comfortably afford to pay for it in cash. Want to take a cruise to the Bahamas? Ditto. Like to impress your neighbors with a brand new big-screen TV? Don't buy it on the "easy-pay" plan. Either pay for it in cash right now (if you can) . . . or keep watching your little TV. And while you're at it, think long and hard about the role that material possessions play in your life—and the role that they should play.

How important are our material possessions? Not as important as we might think. In the lives of committed Christians, material possessions should play a rather small role. Of course, we all need the basic necessities of life, but once we meet those needs for ourselves and for our families, the piling up of possessions creates more problems than it solves. Our real riches, of course, are not of this world. We are never really rich until we are rich in spirit.

> Make up your mind to associate with people who will not pressure you to spend money for things you don't need.

Barbara Johnson observed, "The more we stuff ourselves with material pleasures, the less we seem to appreciate life." How true.

So, if you find yourself wrapped up in the concerns of the material world, it's time to reorder your priorities by turning your thoughts and your prayers to more important matters. And, it's time to begin storing up riches that will endure throughout eternity: the spiritual kind.

It's sobering to contemplate how much time, effort, sacrifice, compromise, and attention we give to acquiring and increasing our supply of something that is totally insignificant in eternity.

Anne Graham Lotz

If you want to be truly happy, you won't find it on an endless quest for more stuff. You'll find it in receiving God's generosity and in passing that generosity along.

Bill Hybels

There is absolutely no evidence that complexity and materialism lead to happiness. On the contrary, there is plenty of evidence that simplicity and spirituality lead to joy, a blessedness that is better than happiness.

Dennis Swanberg

The cross is laid on every Christian. It begins with the call to abandon the attachments of this world.

Dietrich Bonhoeffer

As faithful stewards of what we have, ought we not to give earnest thought to our staggering surplus?

Elisabeth Elliot

For what does it benefit a man to gain the whole world yet lose his life? What can a man give in exchange for his life?

Mark 8:36-37 HCSB

Don't collect for yourselves treasures on earth, where moth and rust destroy and where thieves break in and steal. But collect for yourselves treasures in heaven, where neither moth nor rust destroys, and where thieves don't break in and steal. For where your treasure is, there your heart will be also.

Matthew 6:19-21 HCSB

Anyone trusting in his riches will fall, but the righteous will flourish like foliage.

Proverbs 11:28 HCSB

For the mind-set of the flesh is death, but the mind-set of the Spirit is life and peace.

Romans 8:6 HCSB

Do not love the world or the things in the world. If anyone loves the world, the love of the Father is not in him.

1 John 2:15 NKJV

Can your wealth or all [your] physical exertion keep [you] from distress?

Job 36:19 HCSB

Keeping Up with the Joneses

Do you buy things based upon your needs, or do you buy things based upon your need to impress other people? If you're trying too hard to keep up with the Joneses, you're setting yourself up for a series of headaches, frustrations, and disappointments.

As a member-in-good-standing in this highly competitive, 21st-century world, you know that the demands and expectations of everyday living can seem burdensome, even overwhelming at times. Keeping up appearances (in order to impress your neighbors) can become a fulltime job if you let it. A better strategy, of course, is to stop trying to please the neighbors and to concentrate, instead, upon pleasing God.

Perhaps you have set your goals high; if so, congratulations! That means that you're willing to dream big dreams, and that's a very good thing. But as you consider your life's purpose, don't allow your ambitions to interfere with your desire to please God.

As a believer, your instructions are clear: you must strive to honor God in every facet of your life, and that includes the way that you choose to spend your money. So if you're making purchases in order to keep up with the Joneses—or anybody else—stop it! Pleasing God is more important than impressing your neighbors . . . far more important.

Simplify Your Life

But godliness with contentment is a great gain.
For we brought nothing into the world, and we can take
nothing out. But if we have food and clothing,
we will be content with these. But those who want to be
rich fall into temptation, a trap,
and many foolish and harmful desires,
which plunge people into ruin and destruction.
1 Timothy 6:6-9 HCSB

You live in a world where simplicity is in short supply. Think for a moment about the complexity of your life and compare it to the lives of your ancestors. Certainly, you are the beneficiary of many technological innovations, but these innovations have a price: in all likelihood, your world is highly complex. Consider the following:

1. From the moment you wake up in the morning until the time you lay your head on the pillow at night, you are the target of an endless stream of advertising information. Each message is intended to grab your attention in order to convince you to purchase things you didn't know you needed (and probably don't!).

2. Essential aspects of your life, including personal matters such as health care, are subject to an ever-increasing flood of rules and regulations.

3. Unless you take firm control of your time and your life, you may be overwhelmed by a tidal wave of complexity that threatens your happiness.

Is yours a life of moderation or accumulation? Are you more interested in the possessions you can acquire or in the person you can become? The answers to these questions will determine the direction of your day and, in time, the direction of your life.

If your material possessions are somehow distancing you from God, discard them. If your outside interests leave you too little time for your family or your Creator, slow down the merry-go-round, or better yet, get off the merry-go-round completely. Remember: God wants your full attention, and He wants it today, so don't let anybody or anything get in His way.

Distractions must be conquered or they will conquer us. So let us cultivate simplicity; let us want fewer things; let us walk in the Spirit; let us fill our minds with the Word of God and our hearts with praise.

A. W. Tozer

Prescription for a happier and healthier life: resolve to slow down your pace; learn to say no gracefully; resist the temptation to chase after more pleasure, more hobbies, and more social entanglements.

James Dobson

There is no correlation between wealth and happiness.

Larry Burkett

I am beginning to learn that it is the sweet, simple things of life which are the real ones after all.

Laura Ingalls Wilder

The most powerful life is the most simple life. The most powerful life is the life that knows where it's going, that knows where the source of strength is; it is the life that stays free of clutter and happenstance and hurriedness.

Max Lucado

When Jesus saw it, He was indignant and said to them, "Let the little children come to Me; don't stop them, for the kingdom of God belongs to such as these. I assure you: Whoever does not welcome the kingdom of God like a little child will never enter it." After taking them in His arms, He laid His hands on them and blessed them.

Mark 10:14-16 HCSB

There is one who makes himself rich, yet has nothing; and one who makes himself poor, yet has great riches.

Proverbs 13:7 NKJV

Simplicity Is Beautiful: If your mailbox is overflowing with credit card bills and your bank balance is approaching single digits, it's officially time to simplify your life. But before you unload that seldom-used food processor at your next yard sale, toss your credit cards into the blender and push "Liquefy."

Notes to Yourself About Keeping Up with the Joneses and Simplifying Your Life

On the lines below, assess your susceptibility to peer pressure. And if your overly concerned with impressing your neighbors, ask yourself why. Then, jot down at least ten ways that you can simplify your life.

_____

_____

_____

_____

_____

_____

_____

_____

_____

_____

_____

_____

Principle 10

Plan Carefully for Your Retirement

*Have them gather all the food and grain
of these good years into the royal storehouses,
and store it away . . . .*
Genesis 41:35 NLT

Even if you plan on working fulltime until the day you die, you still need a retirement plan. And while you're planning for the future, don't expect Social Security to provide for your every need. After all, Social Security was designed to provide some financial assistance, but it was never intended to be your only source of retirement income. So, if you're planning on letting Uncle Sam pick up the entire tab for your golden years, you'd better prepare yourself for a very modest lifestyle. A far better strategy, of course, is to start thinking about your retirement long before you retire, and to plan accordingly.

What's your plan for retirement? Are you adding money every year to an IRA? Do you own investment real estate? Do you own mutual funds that match your long-term goals and objectives? Are you building financial reserves month in and month out? And when you do the math, do you have a target age when it seems likely that you'll be able to retire comfortably? If so, keep up the good work. If not, it's time to get serious about your financial future. Now.

A Quick Assessment of Your Retirement Needs

In the space below, please do the following:

1. Jot down the approximate amount of money (in today's dollars) that you think you'll need to retire comfortably.

2. List the secure sources of retirement income that you have already salted away: (IRAs, pension income, investment income, Social Security, etc.).

3. Subtract the income you need to retire (as estimated in #1) from the income you can already identify (the total estimated in #2). This calculation will provide an estimate of the amount of additional monthly income you'll need to create before you can retire comfortably.

1. Amount of Retirement Income You Think You'll Need:

_____

2. Sources of Retirement Income You Can Already Plan On:

Retirement Income Source 1 _____

Retirement Income Source 2 _____

Retirement Income Source 3 _____

Retirement Income Source 4 _____

Total _____

3. Additional Monthly Income You'll Need to Generate Before You Can Retire Comfortably (#1 minus the total of #2): _____

Plan ahead—it wasn't raining when Noah built the ark.

—

Anonymous

Don't Fall for Get-Rich-Quick Schemes

Wealth from get-rich-quick schemes quickly disappears;
wealth from hard work grows.

Proverbs 13:11 NLT

In today's world of lightning-fast communications, get-rich-quick schemes are just about everywhere. Log onto your e-mail and you may find a "radically new" way to double your money in just a few weeks. Such scams are usually too absurd to be believed by any competent adult, yet sometimes these offers are so shrewdly crafted that they may seem believable. Your challenge, if you want to become financially secure, is to invest only in things you understand— and to choose only those investments that have a reasonable likelihood of success. That means that unless you're a trained investment professional, you'll be wise to seek outside guidance from proven professionals whom you trust. And you'll be wise to avoid any investment that seems too good to be true.

The Bible warns time and again against the sin of greed. When we take this warning to heart (by forgoing high-risk, low-common-sense investments), we are rewarded financially and emotionally for our good judgment.

So the next time someone tries to get you to invest in Florida swampland, African diamond mines, or the next "can't-miss penny stock," remember the old adage: Sometimes the best way to double your money is to fold it up and put it in your wallet.

Understand Your Investments: If it sounds too good to be true, it is. If you can't figure out how they're making all that money, they aren't.

Here's a recipe for handling money wisely: Take a heaping helping of common sense, add a sizeable portion of self-discipline, and mix with prayer.

Marie T. Freeman

Know what you own and why you own it.

Peter Lynch

Large enterprises make the few rich, but the majority prosper only through the carefulness and detail of thrift.

T. T. Munger

Virtue—even attempted virtue—brings light; indulgence brings fog.

C. S. Lewis

Wisdom always waits for the right time to act, while emotion always pushes for action right now.

Joyce Meyer

The three great essentials to achieve anything worthwhile are, first, hard work; second, stick-to-itiveness; third, common sense.

Thomas Edison

Diversity Matters

Once you've established a sensible reserve account, then you can start thinking about other investments, including mutual funds, real estate, or other proven assets. As you begin to build your investment portfolio, it's important to stay diversified. That means not putting all, or even most, of your funds into a single investment or category of investments. And while you're at it, leave professional investing to the investment professionals. Don't try to become an amateur day-trader, a weekend stock-picker, or an instant real estate expert. Instead, find professional advisors with great references and proven track records. Then, let them help you build your investment portfolio and diversify your assets.

One Way to Manage Risk Is By Diversifying Your Investments: Having too many eggs in any one investment basket (even if that investment is your own small business) is a formula for financial disappointment.

Think Long Term: If you wish to become a successful saver and an enlightened investor, you will need to exercise patience. If you think you want to be a speculator or a day trader, think again.

Don't Get Greedy: High-risk investments have the potential for high returns, but they also have the potential for no return at all. Unless you happen to be a seasoned pro in the world of finance, you should steer clear of risky "high-yield" investments and stick with safer investments that offer both security and peace of mind. High-risk investments are usually high-stress investments, too. So do yourself a favor: be sensible and safe. It's the smart way to invest and the peaceful way to live.

Use Insurance to Manage Risk

*A prudent person foresees the danger ahead
and takes precautions; the simpleton goes blindly on and
suffers the consequences.*

Proverbs 22:3 NLT

Your world is full of uncertainties; that's why you need insurance. Although you cannot control the future, you can and should plan for it; to do otherwise is to invite havoc into your own life, not to mention the lives of your family members. As you think about your insurance plan, here's a brief introduction to the things you need to know:

Insurance 101:

You Need Insurance. Period. At a minimum, here's what you need:

1. Enough life insurance to provide for your family in the event of your death;

2. Sufficient health insurance to provide for you and for those under your care;

3. Auto insurance (if you own a car);

4. Home insurance (if you own a home) or renter's insurance (to cover your personal possessions).

5. You should also consider purchasing an inexpensive disability policy to augment Social Security benefits.

And, of course, don't hesitate to ask an expert to look at all your insurance needs in detail (this little book is good, but no book is that good!).

Insurance 201:

Shop Around. Over your lifetime, you'll spend a surprisingly large percentage of your income on insurance. Insurance prices are highly variable. To make sure that you're not overpaying, shop around before you buy and when you renew policies.

Insurance 301:

The Great Life Insurance Dilemma—Term Versus Whole Life: Term life insurance is the kind of insurance that provides death benefits only. A "whole life" insurance policy (and other similar types of policies) is, in essence, a term policy with certain additional investment features added on for good measure. For obvious reasons, whole life policies usually cost substantially more than term policies. In most cases, you'll be better off purchasing term insurance (especially if you need lots of insurance at a cheap price). But, whole life policies do have certain advantages, especially if you wish to lock in a particular premium payment for the rest of your life. When in doubt about which type of policy is best for you, check with a professional advisor whom you trust.

Our actions are seen by people,
but our motives
are monitored by God.

—

Franklin Graham

Plan for Your Death

Though I walk through the valley
of the shadow of death, I will fear no evil:
for thou art with me.

Psalm 23:4 KJV

If you've worked hard, worked smart, saved your money, and invested wisely, you won't die broke. Technically, the assets that you own are called your "estate." These assets represent the money left over from your entire life's work. So why not decide where your assets will go? If you don't, the government will certainly decide for you, but that choice should be yours (not the courts'), and that's why you absolutely need a will.

If you die without a will, you may create confusion and hurt feelings among your family members. But a clear, unambiguous will can eliminate the confusion. So, you'll be doing your heirs a huge favor by spelling out your wishes.

If you've accepted Christ as your personal Savior, you're going to live forever . . . in heaven. But you shouldn't neglect earthly duties, either. And that means having a will.

Estate Planning 101:

If you own a home or have other substantial assets that you want to pass on to the next generation, it's best to have a trusted professional help you draft your will so that you can make fully informed decisions about the ultimate distribution of your assets.

Consider a holographic will: If you're planning on hiring a lawyer to draft your will, but you haven't done so yet, you should consider writing a holographic will. What's a holographic will? It's a will that is written in your own handwriting. And if you don't currently have a valid will, perhaps you should consider writing down your wishes right now. A holographic will is no substitute for a well-crafted instrument that has been drafted by a professional. But, a holographic will is almost always better than nothing . . . lots better.

Have a Written Will

Most people die without a will. Don't be like most people. On the lines below, make a list of assets that you will want to include in your will.

_____

_____

_____

_____

_____

_____

_____

_____

_____

_____

_____

_____

_____

_____

An Inventory of Your Insurance

On the lines below, list the insurance policies that you currently own, including health, life, home, auto, disability, and personal liability. If you feel you're not fully protected, you should also jot down the types and amounts of insurance that you should purchase in order to ensure that your coverage is adequate for you and your family.

_____

_____

_____

_____

_____

_____

_____

_____

_____

_____

_____

Principle 11

Expect God's Abundance

I have come that they may have life,
and that they may have it more abundantly.
John 10:10 NKJV

D o you believe that God intends for you to experience abundance here on earth and throughout eternity? Are you optimistic about your future and enthused about the opportunities God has placed before you? You should be. After all, as a believer, you have every reason to be optimistic about your life here on earth and your eternal life in heaven. As English clergyman William Ralph Inge observed, "No Christian should be a pessimist, for Christianity is a system of radical optimism." Inge's words are most certainly true, yet sometimes you may find yourself pulled down by the inevitable concerns of everyday life. When your checkbook is running on empty—or if you find yourself struggling with other money-related problems—you may become discouraged, exhausted, or both. If so, God wants to have a little chat with you. After all, your Heavenly Father has made promises to you that He intends to keep. And if your life has been transformed by God's only begotten Son, then you, as a recipient of God's grace, have every reason to live courageously.

Are you willing to trust God's plans? Hopefully, you will trust Him completely with every facet of your life, including your finances. After all, the words of the Psalmist make it clear: "The ways of God are without fault. The Lord's words are pure. He is a shield to those who trust him" (Psalm 18:30 NCV).

Woodroll Kroll noted, "If our minds are stayed upon God, His peace will rule the affairs entertained by our minds. If, on the other hand, we allow our minds to dwell on the cares of this world, God's peace will be far from our thoughts." These words should serve as a reminder that even when the challenges of the day seem daunting, God remains steadfast. And, so should you.

So make this promise to yourself and keep it—vow to be an expectant, faith-filled Christian. Think optimistically about your life, your profession, your family, your future, and your finances. Trust your hopes, not your fears. Take time to celebrate God's glorious creation. And then, when you've filled your heart with hope and gladness, share your optimism with others. They'll be better for it, and so will you.

Is material abundance part of God's plan for your life? Perhaps. But in every circumstance of life, during times of wealth or times of want, God will provide for you and give you precisely what you need if you trust Him (Matthew 6). So trust Him today, tomorrow, and forever. When you do, His abundance will overflow to you, to your loved ones, and to generations yet unborn.

- Abundance and obedience go hand-in-hand. Obey God first and expect to receive His abundance second, not vice versa.

- Remember that spiritual abundance is more important than material abundance.

- Understand the importance of thanking God for gifts that are simply too numerous to count.

- Think about ways that you can follow Christ more closely and, by doing so, live more abundantly.

Financial abundance, when it is not accompanied by obedience to God's commandments, can be more of a curse than a blessing. Genuine abundance begins with God and His only begotten Son. Make all your plans—including, of course, your financial plans—with God's Word as your compass and God's Son as your guide.

God's riches are beyond anything we could ask or even dare to imagine! If my life gets gooey and stale, I have no excuse.

Barbara Johnson

It would be wrong to have a "poverty complex," for to think ourselves paupers is to deny either the King's riches or to deny our being His children.

Catherine Marshall

If we were given all we wanted here, our hearts would settle for this world rather than the next.

Elisabeth Elliot

People, places, and things were never meant to give us life. God alone is the author of a fulfilling life.

Gary Smalley & John Trent

The only way you can experience abundant life is to surrender your plans to Him.

Charles Stanley

And God is able to make every grace overflow to you, so that in every way, always having everything you need, you may excel in every good work.

2 Corinthians 9:8 HCSB

Until now you have asked for nothing in My name. Ask and you will receive, that your joy may be complete.

John 16:24 HCSB

Come to terms with God and be at peace; in this way good will come to you.

Job 22:21 HCSB

My cup runs over. Surely goodness and mercy shall follow me all the days of my life; and I will dwell in the house of the Lord forever.

Psalm 23:5-6 NKJV

And He said to them, "Take heed and beware of covetousness, for one's life does not consist in the abundance of the things he possesses."

Luke 12:15 NKJV

I am the Alpha and the Omega, the Beginning and the End. I will give to the thirsty from the spring of living water as a gift.

Revelation 21:6 HCSB

Remember That We're Only Stewards

Let a man so consider us, as servants of Christ and stewards of the mysteries of God. Moreover it is required in stewards that one be found faithful.

1 Corinthians 4:1-2 NKJV

Christian stewardship may be defined as "the proper management of one's resources for the glory of God." And, for thoughtful believers, stewardship is the foundation of any financial plan.

As Christians, we are challenged to be faithful stewards of the resources and talents that God has given us. But we live in a world that encourages us to do otherwise. Ours is a society that is filled to the brim with countless opportunities to squander our time, our talents, and our money. Yet we must beware because God has warned us never to squander the blessings that He has bestowed upon us.

All of us have special gifts, and you are no exception. Today, accept this challenge: value the talent that God has given you, nourish it, make it grow, and share it with the world. For dedicated believers like you, stewardship is not something to be taken lightly. After all, God has given you a wide array of opportunities and a special set of abilities.

That's why you must manage your resources as if they were a one-of-a-kind treasure on loan from God, which, by the way, they are.

How will you honor God today? Will you honor Him with the best you have to offer? Will you tithe the firstfruits of your harvest? Will you praise God not only with your words but also with your deeds? If you do, you will be blessed by a loving and righteous Father.

Each day provides a fresh opportunity to honor God with your prayers, with your praise, with your resources, and with your service. Does the level of your stewardship honor the One who has given you everything? If so, rest assured that God will bless you because of your obedience. And if your stewardship has been somehow deficient, the best day to change is this one.

When you become a better steward of the resources God has given you . . . He gives you more resources to manage.

Christians have become victims of one of the most devious plots Satan ever created—the concept that money belongs to us and not to God.

Larry Burkett

If our charities do not at all pinch or hamper us, I should say they are too small. There ought to be things we should like to do and cannot do because our charitable expenditure excludes them.

C. S. Lewis

God will withdraw resources from the poor stewards, as related in Matthew 25, and give it to the good stewards.

Bill Bright

A steward is one who manages another's resources. Each of us is a manager, not an owner. God is the owner, and we are to manage according to His plan.

Larry Burkett

You can sing your heart out but never give back to God, and you'll miss the fullness of worship.

Dave Ramsey

A steward does not own, but instead manages, all that his master puts into his hands.

Warren Wiersbe

Based on the gift they have received, everyone should use it to serve others, as good managers of the varied grace of God.

1 Peter 4:10 HCSB

Every good gift and every perfect gift is from above, and cometh down from the Father of lights.

James 1:17 KJV

His master said to him, "Well done, good and faithful slave! You were faithful over a few things; I will put you in charge of many things. Enter your master's joy!"

Matthew 25:21 HCSB

We have different gifts, according to the grace given us. If a man's gift is prophesying, let him use it in proportion to his faith. If it is serving, let him serve; if it is teaching, let him teach; if it is encouraging, let him encourage; if it is contributing to the needs of others, let him give generously; if it is leadership, let him govern diligently; if it is showing mercy, let him do it cheerfully.

Romans 12:6-8 NIV

Do not neglect the gift that is in you.

—

1 Timothy 4:14 NKJV

Assessing Your Level of Stewardship

In the spaces below, assess yourself in four aspects of stewardship: how you're sharing **your talents**, **your time**, **your money**, and **your testimony**. Then, give yourself an overall grade.

1. How am I using my talents? Am I a good steward of the gifts and opportunities that God has given me? _____

_____

_____

_____

_____

_____

_____

2. Do I make good use of the time God has given me? How might I improve my time management skills? _____

_____

_____

_____

_____

_____

3. Am I a faithful steward of the money God has entrusted to my care? Am I giving God a fair portion of my income? Am I a cheerful giver?

_____

_____

_____

_____

_____

_____

4. Am I willing to share my testimony with others, or am I hesitant to share my faith? _____

_____

_____

_____

_____

_____

_____

5. The overall grade that I give myself for stewardship:

_____

Are You Expecting Abundance?

On the lines below, assess yourself on whether or not you really expect to receive the kind of spiritual abundance that God has promised in John 10:10. While you're at it, define precisely what abundance means to you.

_____

_____

_____

_____

_____

_____

_____

_____

_____

_____

_____

_____

Principle 12

Trust God to Handle Everything, Including Your Finances

Trust in the Lord with all your heart,
and do not rely on your own understanding;
think about Him in all your ways,
and He will guide you on the right paths.
Proverbs 3:5-6 HCSB

As we come to the end of this book, it's worth remembering that God has the final word on everything, including your finances. The Bible contains principles for financial security which, if followed, will lead to long-term financial independence for you and your family. But in order to follow the Bible's instructions, you must take the time to understand the Biblical laws that apply to your own economic well-being. And you must learn to trust God completely, which means trusting Him with your finances, too.

The ideas in this text have been intended to help you revolutionize the way that you think about money and the way that you handle your personal finances. If you take these ideas to heart and apply them to your life, you will live wisely and well, and that's good. But matters of this earth, including your financial well-being, are of no importance when compared with matters of spiritual well-being. So place God at the center of your heart, and trust Christ for your personal salvation. Then, obey God's Word in every aspect of your life. When you do, God will bless you, and you, in turn, will bless others.

Money is a tool, nothing more. It is a tool that can and should be used by you to improve your own life and the lives of your loved ones. If you approach the use of money in a disciplined, thoughtful way, and if you live by God's commandments, you will be surprised at the gifts that He has in store for you. So trust God, obey His commandments . . . and then start unwrapping those gifts!

In whatever circumstance you find yourself, you need never lose hope. Since God is trustworthy—and since He has made promises to you that He intends to keep—you are protected.

A steward is one who manages another's resources. Each of us is a manager, not an owner. God is the owner, and we are to manage according to His plan.

Larry Burkett

When I feel like circumstances are spiraling downward in my life, God taught me that whether I'm right side up or upside down, I need to turn those circumstances over to Him. He is the only one who can bring balance into my life.

Carole Lewis

I believe that in every time and place it is within our power to acquiesce in the will of God—and what peace it brings to do so!

Elisabeth Elliot

Trusting God completely means having faith that he knows what is best for your life. You expect him to keep his promises, help you with problems, and do the impossible when necessary.

Rick Warren

It's not the strength of your faith that's important. It's the object of your faith. If you are trusting God, then you will receive all that God can give you.

Warren Wiersbe

If they serve Him obediently,
they will end their days in prosperity
and their years in happiness.

—

Job 36:11 HCSB

Give Thanks to God and Trust Him Always

Thanks be to God for His indescribable gift.
2 Corinthians 9:15 HCSB

If you're in the midst of building a financial nest egg, then you're undoubtedly striving to create a better life for your loved ones and yourself. But while you're building, do you also slow down every day to thank God for the blessings He has already given you? Hopefully so.

Dietrich Bonhoeffer observed, "It is only with gratitude that life becomes rich." These words most certainly apply to you.

As a follower of Christ, you have been blessed beyond measure. God sent His only Son to die for you. And, God has given you the priceless gifts of eternal love and eternal life. You, in turn, should approach your Heavenly Father with reverence and gratitude.

Are you a thankful person? Do you appreciate the gifts that God has given you? And, do you demonstrate your gratitude by being a faithful steward of the gifts and talents that you have received from your Creator? You most certainly should be thankful. After all, when you stop to think about it, God has given you more blessings than you can count. So the question of the day is this: will you thank your Heavenly Father . . . or will you spend your time and energy doing other things?

God is always listening—are you willing to say thanks? It's up to you, and the next move is yours.

Always Be Thankful

By speaking words of thanksgiving and praise, you honor the Father and you protect your heart against the twin evils of apathy and ingratitude. You owe God everything . . . including your thanks.

The words "thank" and "think" come from the same root word. If we would think more, we would thank more.

Warren Wiersbe

If you can't tell whether your glass is half-empty or half-full, you don't need another glass; what you need is better eyesight . . . and a more thankful heart.

Marie T. Freeman

Thanksgiving or complaining—these words express two contrastive attitudes of the souls of God's children in regard to His dealings with them. The soul that gives thanks can find comfort in everything; the soul that complains can find comfort in nothing.

Hannah Whitall Smith

God has promised that if we harvest well with the tools of thanksgiving, there will be seeds for planting in the spring.

Gloria Gaither

It is only with gratitude that life becomes rich.

Dietrich Bonhoeffer

Therefore as you have received Christ Jesus the Lord, walk in Him, rooted and built up in Him and established in the faith, just as you were taught, and overflowing with thankfulness.

Colossians 2:6-7 HCSB

Enter into His gates with thanksgiving, and into His courts with praise. Be thankful to Him, and bless His name. For the Lord is good; His mercy is everlasting, and His truth endures to all generations.

Psalm 100:4-5 NKJV

And whatever you do, in word or in deed, do everything in the name of the Lord Jesus, giving thanks to God the Father through Him.

Colossians 3:17 HCSB

It is good to give thanks to the Lord, and to sing praises to Your name, O Most High.

Psalm 92:1 NKJV

And let the peace of the Messiah, to which you were also called in one body, control your hearts. Be thankful.

Colossians 3:15 HCSB

50 Things You're Thankful For

On the lines and pages that follow, jot down 50 things you're thankful for. Because God has blessed you in so many ways, this list is only the tip of the iceberg, but it's a start. And while you're counting your blessings, don't forget to thank God for them.

_____

_____

_____

_____

_____

_____

_____

_____

_____

_____

_____

_____

_____

_____

_____

_____

_____

_____

_____

_____

_____

_____

_____

_____

_____

_____

_____

_____

_____

_____

_____

_____

_____

_____

_____

_____

_____

_____

_____

_____

_____

_____

_____

_____

_____

_____

_____

_____

_____

_____

Budget Planning

Budget for the Month of January

Income

Monthly Income #1 (After Tax) = _____

Monthly Income #2 (After Tax) = _____

Interest Income (After Tax) = _____

Other Income (After Tax) = _____

Total Est. Income after Tax = _____

Expenses

Tithing = _____

Monthly Housing Expenses:

Rent/Mortgage Payment = _____

Association Fees = _____

Property Taxes = _____

Homeowner's Insurance = _____

Utilities

    Gas = _____

    Water = _____

    Electric = _____

    Trash Pickup = _____

Home Phone = _____

Cell Phone = _____

Cable TV = _____

Internet = _____

Misc. Home Maintenance = _____

Monthly Car Expenses:

Car Payments = _____

Auto Insurance = _____

Gasoline (Automobile) = _____

Regular Auto Service = _____

Misc. Auto Expenses = _____

Monthly Health Costs and Other Insurance:

Health Insurance = _____

Medicine = _____

Estimated Deductibles = _____

Donations = _____

Life Insurance = _____

Disability Insurance = _____

Other Insurance = _____

Other Monthly Expenses:

Household Supplies = _____

Groceries = _____

School Supplies = _____

Clothing = _____

Entertainment = _____

Travel = _____

Installment Loans = _____

Credit Card Payments = _____

Misc. Out-of-Pocket Expenses = _____

Total Est. Monthly Expenses = _____

Estimated Income After Expenses = _____

Budget for the Month of February

Income

Monthly Income #1 (After Tax) = _____

Monthly Income #2 (After Tax) = _____

Interest Income (After Tax) = _____

Other Income (After Tax) = _____

Total Est. Income after Tax = _____

Expenses

Tithing = _____

Monthly Housing Expenses:

Rent/Mortgage Payment = _____

Association Fees = _____

Property Taxes = _____

Homeowner's Insurance = _____

Utilities

    Gas = _____

    Water = _____

    Electric = _____

    Trash Pickup = _____

Home Phone = _____

Cell Phone = _____

Cable TV = _____

Internet = _____

Misc. Home Maintenance = _____

Monthly Car Expenses:

Car Payments = _____

Auto Insurance = _____

Gasoline (Automobile) = _____

Regular Auto Service = _____

Misc. Auto Expenses = _____

Monthly Health Costs and Other Insurance:

Health Insurance = _____

Medicine = _____

Estimated Deductibles = _____

Donations = _____

Life Insurance = _____

Disability Insurance = _____

Other Insurance = _____

Other Monthly Expenses:

Household Supplies = _____

Groceries = _____

School Supplies = _____

Clothing = _____

Entertainment = _____

Travel = _____

Installment Loans = _____

Credit Card Payments = _____

Misc. Out-of-Pocket Expenses = _____

Total Est. Monthly Expenses = _____

Estimated Income After Expenses = _____

Budget for the Month of March

Income

Monthly Income #1 (After Tax) = _____

Monthly Income #2 (After Tax) = _____

Interest Income (After Tax) = _____

Other Income (After Tax) = _____

Total Est. Income after Tax = _____

Expenses

Tithing = _____

Monthly Housing Expenses:

Rent/Mortgage Payment = _____

Association Fees = _____

Property Taxes = _____

Homeowner's Insurance = _____

Utilities

    Gas = _____

    Water = _____

    Electric = _____

    Trash Pickup = _____

Home Phone = _____

Cell Phone = _____

Cable TV = _____

Internet = _____

Misc. Home Maintenance = _____

Monthly Car Expenses:

Car Payments = _____

Auto Insurance = _____

Gasoline (Automobile) = _____

Regular Auto Service = _____

Misc. Auto Expenses = _____

Monthly Health Costs and Other Insurance:

Health Insurance = _____

Medicine = _____

Estimated Deductibles = _____

Donations = _____

Life Insurance = _____

Disability Insurance = _____

Other Insurance = _____

Other Monthly Expenses:

Household Supplies = _____

Groceries = _____

School Supplies = _____

Clothing = _____

Entertainment = _____

Travel = _____

Installment Loans = _____

Credit Card Payments = _____

Misc. Out-of-Pocket Expenses = _____

Total Est. Monthly Expenses = _____

Estimated Income After Expenses = _____

Budget for the Month of April

Income

Monthly Income #1 (After Tax) = _____

Monthly Income #2 (After Tax) = _____

Interest Income (After Tax) = _____

Other Income (After Tax) = _____

Total Est. Income after Tax = _____

Expenses

Tithing = _____

Monthly Housing Expenses:

Rent/Mortgage Payment = _____

Association Fees = _____

Property Taxes = _____

Homeowner's Insurance = _____

Utilities

    Gas = _____

    Water = _____

    Electric = _____

    Trash Pickup = _____

Home Phone = _____

Cell Phone = _____

Cable TV = _____

Internet = _____

Misc. Home Maintenance = _____

Monthly Car Expenses:

Car Payments = _____

Auto Insurance = _____

Gasoline (Automobile) = _____

Regular Auto Service = _____

Misc. Auto Expenses = _____

Monthly Health Costs and Other Insurance:

Health Insurance = _____

Medicine = _____

Estimated Deductibles = _____

Donations = _____

Life Insurance = _____

Disability Insurance = _____

Other Insurance = _____

Other Monthly Expenses:

Household Supplies = _____

Groceries = _____

School Supplies = _____

Clothing = _____

Entertainment = _____

Travel = _____

Installment Loans = _____

Credit Card Payments = _____

Misc. Out-of-Pocket Expenses = _____

Total Est. Monthly Expenses = _____

Estimated Income After Expenses = _____

Budget for the Month of May

Income

Monthly Income #1 (After Tax) = _____

Monthly Income #2 (After Tax) = _____

Interest Income (After Tax) = _____

Other Income (After Tax) = _____

Total Est. Income after Tax = _____

Expenses

Tithing = _____

Monthly Housing Expenses:

Rent/Mortgage Payment = _____

Association Fees = _____

Property Taxes = _____

Homeowner's Insurance = _____

Utilities

    Gas = _____

    Water = _____

    Electric = _____

    Trash Pickup = _____

Home Phone = _____

Cell Phone = _____

Cable TV = _____

Internet = _____

Misc. Home Maintenance = _____

Monthly Car Expenses:

Car Payments = _____

Auto Insurance = _____

Gasoline (Automobile) = _____

Regular Auto Service = _____

Misc. Auto Expenses = _____

Monthly Health Costs and Other Insurance:

Health Insurance = _____

Medicine = _____

Estimated Deductibles = _____

Donations = _____

Life Insurance = _____

Disability Insurance = _____

Other Insurance = _____

Other Monthly Expenses:

Household Supplies = _____

Groceries = _____

School Supplies = _____

Clothing = _____

Entertainment = _____

Travel = _____

Installment Loans = _____

Credit Card Payments = _____

Misc. Out-of-Pocket Expenses = _____

Total Est. Monthly Expenses = _____

Estimated Income After Expenses =_____

Budget for the Month of June

Income

Monthly Income #1 (After Tax) = _____

Monthly Income #2 (After Tax) = _____

Interest Income (After Tax) = _____

Other Income (After Tax) = _____

Total Est. Income after Tax = _____

Expenses

Tithing = _____

Monthly Housing Expenses:

Rent/Mortgage Payment = _____

Association Fees = _____

Property Taxes = _____

Homeowner's Insurance = _____

Utilities

    Gas = _____

    Water = _____

    Electric = _____

    Trash Pickup = _____

Home Phone = _____

Cell Phone = _____

Cable TV = _____

Internet = _____

Misc. Home Maintenance = _____

Monthly Car Expenses:

Car Payments = _____

Auto Insurance = _____

Gasoline (Automobile) = _____

Regular Auto Service = _____

Misc. Auto Expenses = _____

Monthly Health Costs and Other Insurance:

Health Insurance = _____

Medicine = _____

Estimated Deductibles = _____

Donations = _____

Life Insurance = _____

Disability Insurance = _____

Other Insurance = _____

Other Monthly Expenses:

Household Supplies = _____

Groceries = _____

School Supplies = _____

Clothing = _____

Entertainment = _____

Travel = _____

Installment Loans = _____

Credit Card Payments = _____

Misc. Out-of-Pocket Expenses = _____

Total Est. Monthly Expenses = _____

Estimated Income After Expenses = _____

Budget for the Month of July

Income

Monthly Income #1 (After Tax) = _____

Monthly Income #2 (After Tax) = _____

Interest Income (After Tax) = _____

Other Income (After Tax) = _____

Total Est. Income after Tax = _____

Expenses

Tithing = _____

Monthly Housing Expenses:

Rent/Mortgage Payment = _____

Association Fees = _____

Property Taxes = _____

Homeowner's Insurance = _____

Utilities

    Gas = _____

    Water = _____

    Electric = _____

    Trash Pickup = _____

Home Phone = _____

Cell Phone = _____

Cable TV = _____

Internet = _____

Misc. Home Maintenance = _____

Monthly Car Expenses:

Car Payments = _____

Auto Insurance = _____

Gasoline (Automobile) = _____

Regular Auto Service = _____

Misc. Auto Expenses = _____

Monthly Health Costs and Other Insurance:

Health Insurance = _____

Medicine = _____

Estimated Deductibles = _____

Donations = _____

Life Insurance = _____

Disability Insurance = _____

Other Insurance = _____

Other Monthly Expenses:

Household Supplies = _____

Groceries = _____

School Supplies = _____

Clothing = _____

Entertainment = _____

Travel = _____

Installment Loans = _____

Credit Card Payments = _____

Misc. Out-of-Pocket Expenses = _____

Total Est. Monthly Expenses = _____

Estimated Income After Expenses =_____

Budget for the Month of August

Income

Monthly Income #1 (After Tax) = _____

Monthly Income #2 (After Tax) = _____

Interest Income (After Tax) = _____

Other Income (After Tax) = _____

Total Est. Income after Tax = _____

Expenses

Tithing = _____

Monthly Housing Expenses:

Rent/Mortgage Payment = _____

Association Fees = _____

Property Taxes = _____

Homeowner's Insurance = _____

Utilities

    Gas = _____

    Water = _____

    Electric = _____

    Trash Pickup = _____

Home Phone = _____

Cell Phone = _____

Cable TV = _____

Internet = _____

Misc. Home Maintenance = _____

Monthly Car Expenses:

Car Payments = _____

Auto Insurance = _____

Gasoline (Automobile) = _____

Regular Auto Service = _____

Misc. Auto Expenses = _____

Monthly Health Costs and Other Insurance:

Health Insurance = _____

Medicine = _____

Estimated Deductibles = _____

Donations = _____

Life Insurance = _____

Disability Insurance = _____

Other Insurance = _____

Other Monthly Expenses:

Household Supplies = _____

Groceries = _____

School Supplies = _____

Clothing = _____

Entertainment = _____

Travel = _____

Installment Loans = _____

Credit Card Payments = _____

Misc. Out-of-Pocket Expenses = _____

Total Est. Monthly Expenses = _____

Estimated Income After Expenses =_____

Budget for the Month of September

Income

Monthly Income #1 (After Tax) = _____

Monthly Income #2 (After Tax) = _____

Interest Income (After Tax) = _____

Other Income (After Tax) = _____

Total Est. Income after Tax = _____

Expenses

Tithing = _____

Monthly Housing Expenses:

Rent/Mortgage Payment = _____

Association Fees = _____

Property Taxes = _____

Homeowner's Insurance = _____

Utilities

    Gas = _____

    Water = _____

    Electric = _____

    Trash Pickup = _____

Home Phone = _____

Cell Phone = _____

Cable TV = _____

Internet = _____

Misc. Home Maintenance = _____

Monthly Car Expenses:

Car Payments = _____

Auto Insurance = _____

Gasoline (Automobile) = _____

Regular Auto Service = _____

Misc. Auto Expenses = _____

Monthly Health Costs and Other Insurance:

Health Insurance = _____

Medicine = _____

Estimated Deductibles = _____

Donations = _____

Life Insurance = _____

Disability Insurance = _____

Other Insurance = _____

Other Monthly Expenses:

Household Supplies = _____

Groceries = _____

School Supplies = _____

Clothing = _____

Entertainment = _____

Travel = _____

Installment Loans = _____

Credit Card Payments = _____

Misc. Out-of-Pocket Expenses = _____

Total Est. Monthly Expenses = _____

Estimated Income After Expenses = _____

Budget for the Month of October

Income

Monthly Income #1 (After Tax) = _____

Monthly Income #2 (After Tax) = _____

Interest Income (After Tax) = _____

Other Income (After Tax) = _____

Total Est. Income after Tax = _____

Expenses

Tithing = _____

Monthly Housing Expenses:

Rent/Mortgage Payment = _____

Association Fees = _____

Property Taxes = _____

Homeowner's Insurance = _____

Utilities

    Gas = _____

    Water = _____

    Electric = _____

    Trash Pickup = _____

Home Phone = _____

Cell Phone = _____

Cable TV = _____

Internet = _____

Misc. Home Maintenance = _____

Monthly Car Expenses:

Car Payments = _____

Auto Insurance = _____

Gasoline (Automobile) = _____

Regular Auto Service = _____

Misc. Auto Expenses = _____

Monthly Health Costs and Other Insurance:

Health Insurance = _____

Medicine = _____

Estimated Deductibles = _____

Donations = _____

Life Insurance = _____

Disability Insurance = _____

Other Insurance = _____

Other Monthly Expenses:

Household Supplies = _____

Groceries = _____

School Supplies = _____

Clothing = _____

Entertainment = _____

Travel = _____

Installment Loans = _____

Credit Card Payments = _____

Misc. Out-of-Pocket Expenses = _____

Total Est. Monthly Expenses = _____

Estimated Income After Expenses = _____

Budget for the Month of November

Income

Monthly Income #1 (After Tax) = _____

Monthly Income #2 (After Tax) = _____

Interest Income (After Tax) = _____

Other Income (After Tax) = _____

Total Est. Income after Tax = _____

Expenses

Tithing = _____

Monthly Housing Expenses:

Rent/Mortgage Payment = _____

Association Fees = _____

Property Taxes = _____

Homeowner's Insurance = _____

Utilities

    Gas = _____

    Water = _____

    Electric = _____

    Trash Pickup = _____

Home Phone = _____

Cell Phone = _____

Cable TV = _____

Internet = _____

Misc. Home Maintenance = _____

Monthly Car Expenses:

Car Payments = _____

Auto Insurance = _____

Gasoline (Automobile) = _____

Regular Auto Service = _____

Misc. Auto Expenses = _____

Monthly Health Costs and Other Insurance:

Health Insurance = _____

Medicine = _____

Estimated Deductibles = _____

Donations = _____

Life Insurance = _____

Disability Insurance = _____

Other Insurance = _____

Other Monthly Expenses:

Household Supplies = _____

Groceries = _____

School Supplies = _____

Clothing = _____

Entertainment = _____

Travel = _____

Installment Loans = _____

Credit Card Payments = _____

Misc. Out-of-Pocket Expenses = _____

Total Est. Monthly Expenses = _____

Estimated Income After Expenses = _____

Budget for the Month of December

Income

Monthly Income #1 (After Tax) = _____

Monthly Income #2 (After Tax) = _____

Interest Income (After Tax) = _____

Other Income (After Tax) = _____

Total Est. Income after Tax = _____

Expenses

Tithing = _____

Monthly Housing Expenses:

Rent/Mortgage Payment = _____

Association Fees = _____

Property Taxes = _____

Homeowner's Insurance = _____

Utilities

    Gas = _____

    Water = _____

    Electric = _____

    Trash Pickup = _____

Home Phone = _____

Cell Phone = _____

Cable TV = _____

Internet = _____

Misc. Home Maintenance = _____

Monthly Car Expenses:

Car Payments = _____

Auto Insurance = _____

Gasoline (Automobile) = _____

Regular Auto Service = _____

Misc. Auto Expenses = _____

Monthly Health Costs and Other Insurance:

Health Insurance = _____

Medicine = _____

Estimated Deductibles = _____

Donations = _____

Life Insurance = _____

Disability Insurance = _____

Other Insurance = _____

Other Monthly Expenses:

Household Supplies = _____

Groceries = _____

School Supplies = _____

Clothing = _____

Entertainment = _____

Travel = _____

Installment Loans = _____

Credit Card Payments = _____

Misc. Out-of-Pocket Expenses = _____

Total Est. Monthly Expenses = _____

Estimated Income After Expenses = _____

Budget for the Year of 20____

Income

Monthly Income #1 (After Tax) =   _____

Monthly Income #2 (After Tax) =   _____

Interest Income (After Tax) =   _____

Other Income (After Tax) =   _____

Total Est. Income after Tax =   _____

Expenses

Tithing =   _____

Monthly Housing Expenses:

Rent/Mortgage Payment =   _____

Association Fees =   _____

Property Taxes =   _____

Homeowner's Insurance =   _____

Utilities

    Gas =   _____

    Water =   _____

    Electric =   _____

    Trash Pickup =   _____

Home Phone =   _____

Cell Phone =   _____

Cable TV =   _____

Internet =   _____

Misc. Home Maintenance =   _____

Monthly Car Expenses:

Car Payments = _____

Auto Insurance = _____

Gasoline (Automobile) = _____

Regular Auto Service = _____

Misc. Auto Expenses = _____

Monthly Health Costs and Other Insurance:

Health Insurance = _____

Medicine = _____

Estimated Deductibles = _____

Donations = _____

Life Insurance = _____

Disability Insurance = _____

Other Insurance = _____

Other Monthly Expenses:

Household Supplies = _____

Groceries = _____

School Supplies = _____

Clothing = _____

Entertainment = _____

Travel = _____

Installment Loans = _____

Credit Card Payments = _____

Misc. Out-of-Pocket Expenses = _____

Total Est. Monthly Expenses = _____

Estimated Income After Expenses = _____

**Use these lines to
add budget totals and make notes.**

_____

_____

_____

_____

_____

_____

_____

_____

_____

_____

_____

_____

_____

_____

_____

_____

Money is a training ground
for God to develop
(and for us to discover)
our trustworthiness.
(Luke 16:11)

—

Larry Burkett

Give thanks to the Lord, for He is good;
His faithful love endures forever.

—

Psalm 118:29 HCSB